SilverComm

SilverComm

Marketing Practices and Messages for the Age of Aging

ANNE M. COOPER AND YOUNG JOON LIM

ROWMAN & LITTLEFIELD
Lanham • Boulder • New York • London

Published by Rowman & Littlefield
An imprint of The Rowman & Littlefield Publishing Group, Inc.
4501 Forbes Boulevard, Suite 200, Lanham, Maryland 20706
www.rowman.com

86-90 Paul Street, London EC2A 4NE

British Library Cataloguing in Publication Information Available

Library of Congress Cataloging-in-Publication Data Available

ISBN 9781538175132 (cloth : alk. paper) | ISBN 9781538175149 (pbk. : alk. paper) | ISBN 9781538175156 (ebook)

∞™ The paper used in this publication meets the minimum requirements of American National Standard for Information Sciences—Permanence of Paper for Printed Library Materials, ANSI/NISO Z39.48-1992.

Dedicated to

Dr. Donald Shaw
(1936–2021)

Dr. Michael Sweeney
(1958–2022)

Acknowledgments

The authors gratefully acknowledge the help and support of the following:

Jane Brown
Douglas Cooper
Tricia Currie-Knight
Marilyn Greenwald
Hong Ji
Constance Kehoe
Danese Mabbitt
Rowena Mason
Natalie Mandziuk
Milad Minooie
Linda Mortensen
Yu Ozaki
Staunton, VA, Public Library librarians
Eugene Sandy
Sue Singer Siegel
Henry Tonn
Kevin Weber
Jan Yopp

CHAPTER 1

The Age of Aging

Silver shines with lustrous brilliance; its malleability enhances its beauty; it has value—hence the term *precious metal*; it has a long, storied history, dating back to 4,000 BCE; its commercial importance ranges from dentistry to touch screens (Britannica, n.d.). So, too, the silver wave of the U.S. population: lustrous, flexible, rich in history, important, economically valuable. This older audience has needs that marketers can meet. No, not all people 65 and over have visibly silver (or gray) hair. However, the authors believe that hair color remains a symbol of differentiation between the generations.

Paul Irving of the Milken Institute sees aging as possibly "the greatest challenge of this century" (Llana, 2017, para. 8), whereas Steven Johnson (2021a, p. 15) refers to longevity as "this incredible feat." They articulate two sides of the silver tsunami that has begun to wash over U.S. society. Where Irving sees a challenge, Johnson (2021a, 14–15) emphasizes the positive: "There are few measures of human progress more astonishing than this." In other words, as his PBS series titled *Extra Life* indicates, citizens of the developed world have been given an extra life—that is, in just the past 100 years, not one but two 40-year lives.

Paradoxically, the good news about reduced mortality due to medical innovations could present challenges as the United States deals with a surge in older persons. What social changes will the gray wave bring? Who will care for great-grandma and great-grandpa? Where will they live? What new professions will emerge? (See Boxes 1.1 and 1.2.)

The U.S. silver "tsunami"—from the Japanese, literally "harbor wave," meaning the arrival of an overwhelming quantity of something—has already prompted a rethinking of certain issues. When, for example, is a person is "too old" to work effectively? In 2016, Donald Trump, 70, did not face the age question encountered by a younger Ronald Reagan (69 during his campaign and

Box 1.1.   Non-Medical Silver Tsunami Services

- A Place for Mom: aPlaceforMom.com, 866-403-6931

  - Offers assisted living, memory care, independent living, home care.
  - "Simplifies the process of finding senior living with customized guidance . . . at no cost to your family, as we're paid by our participating communities and providers."

- AmeriCare HomeCare: americareinfo.com, 866-228-8548

  - In-home caregivers for permanent help or recovery from a procedure, including exercise and pet care. Headquartered in Atlanta, the company has locations in 12 states.

- Carefull: getcarefull.com, 833-836-0050

  - "The money service for safer living. . . . Carefull Guard. Smart money protection built for older adults."

- CarePatrol: www.carepatrol.com

  - Helps families find assisted living and other options for seniors at no cost to families.
  - "Receive a generous commission each time a client chooses one of our providers' services."
  - Franchise buy-in, $77,970–$99,870

- Caring Transitions: Caringtransitions.com, 844-220-5427

  - Offers relocation, downsizing/decluttering, estate sales and online auctions in every state except North Dakota.
  - "Your total solution for peace of mind and minimizing stress."
  - (Independent, local senior transition services exist throughout the United States. Local contractors can customize bathrooms, cabinetry and stair climbers to enable aging in place.)

- Holleran Consulting: holleranconsult.com, 800-941-2168

  - Customer engagement and satisfaction, including resident surveys, at not-for-profit senior living venues and community health organizations. Locations in Wrightsville, PA, and Westminster, CO.

- Home Instead: homeinstead.com, 888-331-3242

  - Provides non-medical companionship, personal care, light housekeeping, transportation and meal prep in one's own home. Headquarters in Omaha, NE, oversees more than 700 franchise locations. Franchise investment amounts to $125,000–$135,000.

- Retirement Planning: RetirementPlanning.net
  - Offers personalized advice for portfolio size of 100K and above.
  - "We custom match and send you profiles of 2 to 3 advisors that match your specific needs."
- Road Scholar (formerly Elderhostel): roadscholar.org, 800-454-5768
  - "The not-for-profit leader in educational travel programs since 1975, offers 6,500 learning adventures." Has programs for 50-plus adults, plus grandparent-grandchild tours.
- Senior Law Counsel: seniorcarecounsel.com, 844-412-4222
  - "Elder law attorneys specialize in advising seniors and their families on a wide variety of legal and financial issues that are unique to the elderly, including how to protect their life savings in the face of long-term care."

Box 1.2. Rent-a-Back: A Literary Silver Tsunami Service

In Anne Tyler's (2018) novel *A Patchwork Planet*, narrator/main character Barnaby Gaitlin works for a company that, as he explains, provides "a service for people who are old or disabled. Any load you can't lift, any chore you don't feel up to, why, just call on us" (p. 12).

Barnaby had certain favorites among his clients: "the unstoppable little black grandma" whose children would call Rent-a-Back when their mother planned something too ambitious, like washing all her upstairs windows by herself; or Maud May, "who smoked cigarettes in a long ivory holder and drank martinis by the quart"; or Mr. Shank (less a favorite than an example of a weirdo), "a lonesome and pathetic type" who tended to call in the middle of the night requesting immediate help for small, non-urgent tasks (p. 55).

Mrs. Dibble, the founder, CEO and communications director of this successful company, gave clients her own number for after-hours emergencies. She handled all scheduling, as well as difficult situations, such as a client's accusation that Barnaby had stolen the cash she kept in her flour bin. Mrs. Dibble, herself a senior, a "dainty, fluttery lady" with surprising physical strength, took as her motto, "We're the muscles, not the brains" (p. 23).

From Mrs. Alford to Mrs. Gordoni to Mrs. Glynn, Pulitzer Prize–winner Tyler, a master at creating quirky characters, does not portray the senior clients of Rent-a-Back in a maudlin or stereotypical way. Aside from their physical decline, the seniors in *A Patchwork Planet* have more individuality than commonality.

Box 1.3.   Silver Tsunami Timeline

1935—Social Security established; average U.S. life expectancy was 62 (Infoplease, n.d.).

1960—Only 9% of the U.S. population was over 65 (Statista, 2021).

1961—President Dwight Eisenhower hosted the first White House Conference on Aging.

1966—Americans older than 64 outnumbered those under age 5 (Ritchie, 2019).

1981—The once-a-decade White House Conference on Aging used quotas for the first time to ensure representation of subgroups.

1989—First Walk to End Alzheimer's is held.

1998—Senator John Glenn, age 77, became the oldest person to travel in space.

2011—The first of U.S. Baby Boomers (born 1946–1964) reached 65.

2020—U.S. life expectancy reached nearly 80 (Arias, Tejada-Vera, & Ahmad, 2021).

2021—The United Nations declared the next 10 years the Decade of Healthy Aging (Jenkins, 2022).

2026—The first of U.S. Baby Boomers (born 1946–1964) will reach 80.

2030—The U.S. 65 and over population will reach 20%—super-aged status (Vespa, 2019).

2044—The last U.S. Baby Boomers will reach 80.

when he took office in 1981). In 2021, Joe Biden, the oldest person to take the oath as U.S. president at age 78, ushered in a whole new perspective on maturity.

Considering that birth rates are falling along with increases in longevity, seniors (with fewer grandchildren) will have decreased demands on their resources and increased wealth at their disposal (Herships, 2016). The U.S. birth rate fell 4% in 2020, according to a government report (Stobbe, 2021)—the lowest point in more than 100 years—that is, since statistics were tracked. The 2020 fertility is half of the fertility of the early 1960s: 56 children per 1,000 women.

Life expectancy, which remained flat throughout most of humankind's history, zoomed up in the past century. (See Box 1.3). In 2021, more than 54 million Americans were 65 or older, as post–World War II Baby Boomers became senior citizens; by 2030 that number will rise to 74 million. The growth of the 65-and-older population contributed to an increase in the national median age from 37.2 years in 2010 to 38.4 in 2019, according to the U.S. Census Bureau's Population Estimates (2020).

Given that the first of the 78 million U.S. Baby Boomers (born 1946–1964) turned 75 in 2021 (Southeast Discovery, n.d.), a common age for moving into a retirement facility, what accommodations can they find and afford? Living arrangements in their final years will affect not only seniors themselves, but society at large. (See chapter 7.) Many of the Silent Generation (born 1922 to 1945) have already decided on or moved to their future living venues.

Generational Cohorts

Researchers from a variety of academic disciplines (Berraies et al., 2017; Melo et al., 2019; Robinson et al., 2013) have used sociologist Karl Mannheim's (1949) generation theory, which posits that those in each category are influenced by the historical, social and cultural events of their adolescence. The cohorts who have now fully (Silent Generation) or partially (Baby Boomers) reached age 65 share certain traits.

The Silent Generation, also called traditionalists, is the oldest generation. They have a desire to work within the social and cultural system rather than to change it, given that they began life under difficult conditions, including the Great Depression, and lived through economic and political uncertainties (World War II and the Cold War). As a result, this generation tends to keep their thoughts to themselves, stay away from activist social movements and avoid conflict resulting from personal confrontation (Lissitsa and Kagan, 2022; Metcalf, 2016). They prefer to work in a hierarchically organized structure led by command-and-control leadership that relies on formal, one-on-one communication with an emphasis on rules and structure (Appold, 2017).

The Baby Boomers is the large group born into prosperity after World War II. They have characteristics of self-assuredness, team orientation, competitiveness and discipline. Their formative political and social circumstances include the civil rights movement, the women's liberation movement, rising divorce rates, enhanced educational opportunities and a workaholic culture (Fingerman et al., 2012; Giles, 2020). While Baby Boomers brought significant changes to U.S. families and companies—they made up one-third of the workforce as of 2018—this generation ranks as among the best business leaders in the world "because of their ability to conduct business responsibly and ethically," which originated from their disciplined parents' belief in hard work and education (Melo et al., 2019, p. 837). Rapidly increased use of technologies, weakened norms governing international relations and shortcomings of authority invoke in this generation a slight distrust of government and corporations, although they as workaholics value face-to-face communication, prefer teamwork collaboration and respect group decision-making. Baby Boomers appreciate "formal and direct communications with a preference for using face-to-face, phone and email" channels while valuing background information and details (Jenkins, 2022, para. 6).

Table 1.1.   Generations by Age

	Year of Birth	Ages in 2022
Gen Z	1997–2012	10–25
Millennials	1981–1996	26–41
Gen X	1965–1980	42–57
Baby Boomers II	1956–1964	58–66
Baby Boomers I	1946–1955	67–76
Silent	1922–1945	77–100

These two cohorts represent the oldest of the five generational groups that share particular beliefs, attitudes, opinions and actions with members of their age cohort. Based on multiple analyses by the Pew Research Center (2015) and the U.S. Census Bureau (2014), Table 1.1 shows the birth years and ages of the generations this book uses in 2022.

Despite the fact that no clearly defined age to "become" a U.S. senior citizen exists, we can consider age 62 for Social Security benefits or age 65 for Medicare as a socially accepted norm for entering senior status. According to a 2020 press release by the U.S. Census Bureau, the 65-and-older population has grown rapidly since 2010, driven by the first Baby Boomers; in 2019, the number of those 65 years old showed a rapid increase (see https://www.census.gov).

MARKETING TO SENIORS

In terms of keeping up with the demand of senior citizens' essentials, Meiners and Seeberger (2010) point out that organizations should stop ignoring the senior market, which used to be stereotyped as "a unique segment of low net-worth individuals dependent on their children's income" (p. 294). Instead, they should develop elder care–driven marketing skills and communication strategies targeting senior citizens with a focus of "all entrepreneurial activities on the relevant markets, industries and consumer groups" (p. 297).

U.S. seniors make 50% of all consumer purchases, but a mere 10% of marketing budgets is allocated to them; in comparison, 50% goes to marketing to millennials (Geller, 2019). Robert Passikoff, president of Brand Keys, Inc., advised marketers to stop missing out on the opportunity of doing business with senior citizens:

> While the millennials are sharing stuff, boomers are buying stuff. If you are a brand, you are in business to make money, and a tweet or share or laugh online doesn't translate into actual bottom-line

dollars. . . . Boomers are an audience that's worth pursuing in virtually every category (Morrissey, 2017, para. 27–28)

Morrissey (2017) reported that corporations in the fields of technology, automobile, travel, condos and sports lost their best opportunity to capitalize on seniors' purchasing power because they wrongly stereotyped "the forgotten generation," with its huge discretionary income, as "out of touch and not interested in the latest gadgets" (para. 6–15). Instead, many corporations invested major marketing resources into future-consumer millennials, reasoning that securing them early could result in lifelong, loyal customers. However, the senior generation has been recognized by brands and corporations as a rising target audience since the mid-2010s. As applied to the senior generation, marketing—defined as "market-oriented company management"—needs to focus on promotional strategies with regard to all relevant senior-market industries and consumer groups (Meiners & Seeberger, 2010, p. 297).

Without a doubt, marketers used to turn their noses up at the "too old" or "stuck in the past" generation until the mid-2010s. In the old days, when views of seniors as "being past their prime, stuck in their ways, and unattractive to marketers" were socially accepted, few saw seniors' potential to be the dominant purchasers (*U.S. News*, 2015, p. 2). As a result, a relatively small number of organizations focused on marketing promotions for a limited number of senior-related products such as life insurance, medical devices and reverse mortgages. However, a wealth of research has helped to turn the tide of organizations' and brand marketers' ignorance. For example, CHPA.org, a U.S. coalition of home and community-based health care organizations, discovered that senior citizens, as a large and influential consumer group, have common characteristics and behaviors (CHPA, 2020, p. 2):

- Concern with living an active and healthy lifestyle
- Motivation to purchase self-care products that engender health and the ability to age in place
- Purchasing of nutritional supplements and technologies that empower independence
- Shopping online just as much as Millennials and have more disposable income and purchasing power
- Holding $2.6 trillion in buying power in the United States
- Consuming products that feature customization, value, experience, simplicity, and convenience.

In sum, the senior generation, who see age as just a number, are not "sitting at home wondering how to connect to the Wi-Fi and counting the minutes until they take their next round of pills" (Geller, 2019, para. 7). Instead, they are enthusiastically involved in a wide range of outside and social activities while controlling 70% of the U.S. disposable income. When targeting these wealthy consumers, corporations and brand marketers are advised to avoid illustrating images of older people sitting around while using a product (Purtill, 2021). More importantly, seniors, "once they have connected with a brand," tend to stay loyal for years with more disposable income, time and a desire to spend money, Scott Gulbransen, director of communications for AARP Nevada, told the *New York Times* (Morrissey, 2017). They also on many occasions are likely to make a purchasing decision for their children and even parents (Tahmincioglu, 2021).

Psychology and Terminology

A Pew survey revealed that younger people see age 60 as old, but those in their 60s see 74 as old; thus people over 50 often try to distance themselves from their age group to avoid negative stereotypes (Chopik et al., 2018). As people tend to think of themselves as being approximately 10 years younger or 20% younger than they actually are, many seniors still go out for fun and live full lives while debunking the concept that aging is a constraint on their ability to pursue things that make them happy (Giffin, 2021). Bruce Horovitz, 69, a freelance journalist for *ABC News*, argued that the gray-haired group of Boomers and beyond is likely to have a hard time accepting the realities of aging while trying to redefine what aging is and what old age looks like (2019). Seniors interviewed by Horovitz (2019) also said that they feel about 10 years younger and feel like they did in their 40s.

Words such as "old" and "elderly" are considered derogatory in American culture (Purtill, 2021). The key to successful marketing to senior citizens is simply not to say "old" or "elder" as part of a seismic shift in the way organizations target senior consumers. In fact, age should never be mentioned in any marketing strategies aimed at older customers, as senior citizens regard 60 as the new 40 (Hughes, 2020).

Thomas Cole, 70, a gerontologist, told the *Wall Street Journal*: "We live in an ageist culture, and we have negative associations with words and images of old people." Indeed, the American Geriatrics Society has stopped using the word "elderly" (Hughes, 2020, para. 10–18). Since people in the mid-60s to early 70s demographic show a tendency to refuse to think of themselves as "old" or to "recognize themselves in the version of old [often] presented," a marketing expert offered a new approach to visualizing senior marketing in a *New York Times* interview: "A 65-year-old and a 25-year-old could be as excited and engaged in life, or an 80-year-old could be running marathons" (Purtill, 2021, para. 19–22).

Technology

While senior citizens dislike words describing them as "old" and "elder," they also abhor another stereotype: the tech-phobic generation. According to Nielsen (2019), a global marketing research firm, seniors are the second-heaviest users of the internet, and more than half of Boomers are on Facebook (2019). Many U.S. senior citizens over 65 communicate with their children and grandchildren, using face-to-face video chat apps on their smartphones; especially during the COVID-19 era, they turned to Zoom to connect with friends (Holpuch, 2020). Their newfound digital lifestyle reflects their willingness to adopt and adapt to smartphone chatting apps and online video conferencing.

According to a study conducted by Pew Research Center (2015), once senior citizens were adept at the internet, most of them made online activities a standard part of their daily routine, although one-third of them struggled to understand newer communication technology. Those in their 60s have friends on Facebook and order on Amazon for deliveries to their houses. Holpuch (2020) pointed out senior citizens' adaptability to the new virtual routines, including online bill paying, grocery orders and restaurant deliveries during the 2020 pandemic year. In other words, they did not avoid developing the digital skills to facilitate life in the COVID reality. A 2021 report by the Holding Co. and Pivotal Ventures discovered that seniors have an increased level of overall use and savviness when it comes to technology: "75% of seniors are using the internet, 53% of seniors own a smartphone and 59% of seniors have broadband access" (Famakinwa, 2021, para. 16). Given that the coronavirus lockdowns have prompted more senior citizens to embrace new communication survival skills, senior techno-phobia has proved to be a myth. In fact, most in their mid-60s were already using Facebook and doing online shopping before the pandemic, while those in their 70s are willing to learn how to navigate devices that can help them, connecting them to their family, to their friends and to the world (Famakinwa, 2021). This phenomenon should lead marketers to invest more resources in using multichannel media on- and offline if they want to reach the majority of senior consumers.

Global Aging

Other nations already confront the mixed blessing of longevity (see Box 9.2). In the Chinese mainland, for example, its approximately 168 million people aged 65 and over constitute the world's largest senior population—larger than the number of people of all ages in Mexico (World Bank, n.d.a; World Bank n.d.b); moreover, China's fertility rate remained less than replacement level, despite abandonment in 2016 of the long-standing one-child policy (Wee & Myers, 2020). However, by far the grayest society in the world is Japan, a country that presents lessons for nations approaching super-aged status.

Japan

On January 5, 2022, Kane Tanaka had a birthday—her 119th. Tanaka thus kept her status as the world's oldest person until her death on April 19, 2022. Nabi Tajima, who died in 2018 at age 117, stands out as the world's last known person to be born in the 19th century. Jiroemon Kimura, who died in 2012 at the age of 116 years, ranks as the oldest man in history.

Japan, which annually celebrates Respect for the Aged Day, can count among its citizens (as of September 2022) more than 90,000 centenarians—88.6% of them women; the number of centenarians per capita in the United States is less than half of Japan's rate. By 2025, Japanese citizens over age 65 will account for 30% of the population, making the country's experience "a topic of interest for other graying industrialized nations following Japan into uncharted demographic territory" (Martin, 2019). Indeed, Japan is a "society older than any in the history of the world" (Bartel, 2015, p. 200).

By 2065, there will be only 1.3 workers per each senior citizen (from 2.3 per senior in 2015). This dearth of younger people means that the Japanese government has "committed to accepting limited numbers of immigrants to handle vital work such as caring for the elderly" (Dooley, 2019)—a significant move for this insular and homogeneous society. In fact, the "Japanese appear far more comfortable with allowing robots rather than foreigners to do the work that a missing generation of young people would do" (Runciman, 2018, p. 22). See Figure 1.1.

PRODUCTS

Japan, which has pursued robotics development since the 1970s, presents an object lesson for Western nations. Indeed, robotic care support products

Figure 1.1. This robot dog exemplifies the increase in robotic elder-care support products, a category that includes vacuum cleaners and food deliverers. *Source:* **Flickr/ MIKI Yoshihito: 6th Generation Aibo. (CC BY 2.0)**

already perform many household tasks (Prieler & Kohlbacker, 2016), such as vacuuming, bringing food to persons with limited mobility and providing companionship—most famously by those inanimate media stars, Japanese robot dogs called Aibos (Adams, 2019). Other aging-related products include those related to *daiojo,* or "peaceful death" (Bartel, 2015, p. 201). When still relatively healthy, elders can buy easy-to-use devices such as phones with large keyboards (Prieler & Kohlbacker, 2016).

Some products that accommodate elders' needs can create as well as solve problems. Already more adult diapers than baby diapers are sold in Japan, and the volume of these diapers—almost 1.5 million tons annually—"looms alongside labor shortages in nursing homes and insufficiently funded pension systems" (Rich & Inoue, 2021) as critical issues. At one rehab facility, 80% of residents need diapers, resulting in 400 pounds of waste per day. One plant recycles the diapers into pellets that can be burned to heat water.

GROWTH SECTOR: SENIOR HOUSING

Traditionally in Japan, it "was considered shameful for the family to commit their elderly to institutional care" (Auestad, 2009, p. 224). However, the days when seniors lived with extended families have all but vanished (Naoi, 1996), partly because the "housewives [who] have been the main care-givers" now work outside the home (Kubota & Babazono, 1997, p. 31) and partly because of women "seeing their male siblings, who have not participated in the care of parents, assuming equal rights to inheritance" (Auestad, 2009, p. 224).

Japan's 9,600 public nursing homes have large waiting lists due to their minimal cost. By contrast, at the private elder care facilities, "the price can be high" (Brasor & Tsukuba, 2014), but still the private senior care market is booming. Marketing is done by the private housing sector, since government-run nursing homes need not market themselves. Most (75%) of such firms operate just one facility (Aizawa, 2014). Companies that oversee multiple facilities have often developed from seemingly unrelated roots. Sompo, the largest operator of fee-based nursing homes in Japan (with more than 25,000 rooms), branched out from its 130-year-old property and casualty insurance business. In 2018, it created four regional headquarters to coordinate its 1,000 offices (Sompocare, 2019). Watami, a restaurant chain, added housing to its food-based origins (Brasor & Tsukuba, 2014). Benesse, a publisher of educational materials and the parent company of Berlitz language schools, moved from issuing correspondence courses for those seeking certification to work at elder-care facilities to operating the facilities themselves; it offers five different types of facilities (Benesse, 2019).

Operated by Community Net, the 13 Yui Maru properties offer service apartments for independent seniors aged 60 or older. The 2011 revision of the law regulating senior housing meant startups could get government subsidies for barrier-free, comfortably large (at least 25 square meters) units. At one Yui Maru village, 80% of the tenants are single women (Martin, 2019). As another alternative, villages in shrinking rural venues such as the Share Kanazawa experiment might take hold. Japan has 8.2 million empty homes and buildings, a number the Nomura Research Institute says will grow to 21.7 million by 2033 (Johnston, 2016).

Japanese and U.S. cultures differ (Hofstede, 2001), but both need places for elders to live, ways to care for their physical needs and amenities to preserve quality of life. It happens that Japan has faced these challenges before other countries (Ji et al., 2021), but aging is a global phenomenon (United Nations, 2019).

Global Comparisons

Second to Japan in its percent of elderly (65 and older) is Italy, at 23%, followed by eight other European nations. In a comparative cross-cultural study at the dawn of the cyber age, Cooper-Chen (2004) studied over-65s' internet usage by surveying their grandchildren in four Asian countries and the United States. She found similarities within Asia—that is, limited internet usage by elders—compared with a rather high level of U.S. usage (one-third of elders).

The United States, now 17% elderly (World Bank, n.d.a), will not exceed 20% until 2030 (Vespa, 2019), but when it does, the ramifications will be monumental. Already a plethora of service businesses have emerged (see Box 1.1). We can learn about the realities of longevity from professionals who work in the field of gerontology communication through the interviews set forth in chapter 2. They will be joined in the future by legions of others in the growing SilverComm sector.

Chapter 1. Projects and Exercises

1. Think about what age should be considered as "old." What benchmark age do you see as a threshold to elder status? Interview various age cohorts about this question. Analyze and compare the opinions.
2. Interview a number of older people you know (including relatives) regarding the changes online and social media have made in their lives.
3. Look up news coverage of the death of the world's oldest person, Kane Tanaka, on April 19, 2022, in Japan. What media outlets did not cover her death? Of those that did, what themes emerged?
4. Conduct research on countries expected to be super-aged by 2030. How will such countries affect the global economy?
5. Discuss some advantages and disadvantages of having a great number of old people in a society after watching TV shows featuring senior characters (see Appendix B).

Part I

WORKING IN SILVERCOMM

CHAPTER 2

Professional Paths

When Matthew King graduated in 2003 with a degree in public relations and mass communication, working with the old people was the last thing he wanted to do. Unlike elders themselves, "younger people tend to have a more defined idea of what old age is like" (Bradley & Longino, 2001, p. 17).

"I thought I would go to Philly and work for a large corporation," King recalls (personal communication, August 10, 2021). After trying radio work, even selling insurance, King got a public relations job with a behavioral health facility; he has stayed in the health field ever since, gaining his MBA along the way. At the end of March 2021, he joined Foundations Health Solutions, locating not in a city like Philadelphia but in the semi-rural Ohio area where he grew up and went to college. "Now I can't imagine doing anything else," he states.

SilverComm professionals like King, Foundations' district director of business development, have taken varied paths to arrive at their current positions. In this chapter, practitioner interviewees will reflect on their philosophies about, the challenges of and the rewards gained from their positions. Their work involves three types of residential venues and two organizations, all of which focus on seniors. While geographically specific, the narratives nevertheless have general relevance.

Nursing Homes

Foundations Health Solutions, the largest chain of skilled nursing facilities (SNFs) in Ohio, manages 59 facilities in that state. The marketing and admissions coordination for three of those falls to Matthew King, liaison for Hickory Creek in The Plains (114 beds), Waterview Pointe in Marietta (67 beds) and

17

Rockland Ridge in Belpre (84 beds), all three of which he tries to visit every week.

A nursing home is "a place for people who can't be cared for at home and need 24-hour nursing care" (Centers for Medicare and Medicaid Services, n.d.a). This level of care, often but not exclusively serving elders, must be licensed to operate under state laws (Law Insider, n.d.). Medicare covers up to 100 days in a SNF (pronounced "sniff" by those in the field), for each benefit period (Centers for Medicare and Medicaid Services, n.d.b). To have Medicaid pay for such care beyond 100 days, a person must give up his or her income, except for minimal personal-needs funds, with the exact amount based on the state guidelines where the person lives (Medicaid Interactive, n.d.).

As of 2016, U.S. nursing homes numbered 15,600—most of them (69.3%) for profit and often expensive; one nursing home in Virginia, for example, costs $9,000 per month. These facilities had 1.7 million licensed beds (CDC, n.d.). Practitioners in this field speak of "need-driven versus choice-driven admissions"; in the latter case, facilities have "begun to aggressively market their organizations" (Chies, 2022, p. 97).

"There is lots of competition in this field," relates King, who either in person or remotely covers Southeast Ohio and parts of West Virginia, meeting with social workers at local hospitals. "We do bedside selling" by meeting with family members and patients about to be discharged from a hospital but not able to go home. "Our goal is to be top of mind, to be the problem solver, if the patient needs dialysis or a CPAP [oxygen machine]."

King speaks at local service clubs, chambers of commerce and senior centers, in order to "get the word out. You can brand [such as via Facebook testimonials], but the local market is golden." To that end, King helps sponsor local golf tournaments, a football homecoming and the local Alzheimer's Relay for Life. He even "calls Bingo games"—and "mows lawns, makes beds."

On July 5, 2021, for the ribbon cutting of the newly opened Rockland Ridge facility, King and others arranged for a football coach and the mayor to attend, while lining up local media coverage. "We got restaurants to make their signature dishes for a Taste of Belpre feature. A local winery even rebranded one of their wines for the opening by putting our logo on the bottle."

"Good marketing folks are hard to find. The pay range is good," he concludes. Now his college-age son, having seen his dad's career blossom, wants to go into long-term-care marketing or some aspect of health care himself.

One organization in touch with providers of aging services, LeadingAge (see below), counts 2,200 nonprofit nursing homes among its 5,000-plus members (about 25% of all nursing homes are not for profit). According to Lisa Sanders, director of media relations for LeadingAge (personal communication, July 20,

2021), nursing homes' "approaches [to communication] vary widely, depending on organization size, resources and priorities," as well as geography.

Chies (2022, p. 456) agrees; some long-term care providers "hire marketing managers and perhaps several assistants to do the marketing. Others combine marketing with public relations and even with other administrative functions. Still others contract with a marketing firm to either advise them or actually do the marketing."

Assisted Living Facilities

Compared to nursing homes, fewer assisted living facilities have nonprofit status; by far the majority (81.0%) had for-profit ownership (CDC, 2019). Assisted living is a "confusing" term that "includes all types of group settings" (Robinson, n.d., p. 11). As of 2016, the U.S. assisted living (residential care) communities numbered 28,900, encompassing 811,500 residents. Marketing at these assisted living venues involves sales, but staff also carry out other functions.

Brightview Senior Living, headquartered in Baltimore, created its first community in Maryland in 1999. Its sister company, The Shelter Group, a real estate management and development firm, began in 1982, focusing on multifamily rentals. Marilyn Duker, the Brightview CEO, became "employee No. 1" at The Shelter Group upon its inception in 1982 (Regan, 2019).

The southernmost venue in the 40-facility Brightview chain, located in the Shenandoah Valley of Virginia, has 87 apartments in its independent living building, as well as accommodations for 30 in the assisted living section and 24 in the memory care (dementia) section. Marketing for the three types of residences differs, with most emphasis on independent living, given that this level is a personal choice—perhaps reluctantly made.

"Independent living is not need-driven," explains Michelle Bradley, sales director at Brightview Baldwin Park in Staunton, VA. "There will be multiple visits [before a move is decided on]. Sometimes research by a family member is first, and then mom will come for a visit. Or sometimes the prospect comes first and then says, 'I want to bring my daughter to see this.' We know they are serious when they bring in family members" (personal communication, July 7, 2021).

Brightview offers a stay-cation for people who want to try the independent living apartments. As respite for caregivers, the assisted living and dementia sections offer respite whereby the person needing care can move in for perhaps two weeks at Brightview. Permanent move-in for those two sections often results "when a crisis occurs"; those new residents tend to be older than

Figure 2.1. The marketing staff at an independent/assisted living venue sent this invitation to older persons who live near the facility, offering to deliver to them complimentary chili during winter 2022. Senior residences' marketing efforts often involve food.

independent-living arrivals. However, two of Brightview's oldest residents, at age 100 and 101, live in the independent building.

Since 90% of Brightview's arrivals come from the local area, marketing relies heavily on locally accessible events, usually involving food and drink (see

Figure 2.1). Some, such as a patio social hour, involve all 40 facilities in the chain, so that corporate headquarters in Baltimore creates a single set of ads and Facebook postings. Others, locally conceived, are planned by Bradley and sales associate Angie Via, such as a July 1 "Brightview Celebrates Independence. Get Your Piece of the Pie" free pie pickup. Brightview also gives away pies at Thanksgiving.

"For our pie event at Thanksgiving, we use local bakers. The number has increased year by year, so that last year we had hundreds of people drive up to get their pie," relates Via. "We thank referrals and businesses in this way" (personal communication, July 7, 2021).

Brightview's senior vice president for technology and marketing, Julie Masiello, has made at least one visit to Brightview Baldwin Park. Masiello, who has had marketing experience in insurance and banking, joined Brightview in June 2016 as vice-president for sales and marketing, rising to senior vice president in 2018. Previously she even for a time owned a children's gym. "The [Baltimore] home office is very accessible," says Bradley regarding headquarters.

Bradley, who has been with Brightview Baldwin Park for 17 years, attends the corporate leadership conference once a year in Maryland. She works with other sales directors, who number about 100—especially interacting with those closest geographically, discussing "problems solved, successes."

One idea that has worked involves resident ambassadors who help with marketing, having lunch with prospects or showing them the resident ambassador's apartment. "It's good to hear from a peer, not from Michelle or me," says Via. "Someone their own age [has credibility]."

Initial visits, which can include walk-ins, number more than 10 in a typical week, post-COVID. "People are more comfortable now. Vaccinations are up. They are realizing that isolation was a problem and see the need for socializing— bridge, church," says Via. "A family member may have had to step in, seeing the decline [of a family member, for example due to the restrictions of COVID] and felt a need to have The Conversation."

Via, an education major who has had experience as a social worker, joined Bradley several years ago. A communication mantra, SPICE, stands for five types of fulfillment that Brightview strives to impart to residents: Spiritual, Physical, Intellectual, Cultural and Emotional.

The sales duo works with other staff members to put together the calendar. For example, once a month Brightview provides "goodies" to local persons who have a connection to the venue. Other tangible swag includes a gift for each visiting family, such as a mug or baked treats.

Via's normal day ("I'm an early bird") begins with prepping those gifts, after she turns on the music and lights in the library and fitness center. A constant concern is checking the database of prospects and future residents. Bradley's day begins with a "stand-up" meeting of all the venue's directors ("We have a family coming at 12:30. Please say hello."). Either one or the other of the sales duo remains in the office, available to take phone calls.

Bradley and Via use phone calls more than emails to follow up with prospects.

They may even deliver a meal to a prospect's home so that they can sample the cuisine. About 90% of residents move in from nearby locations, about a 20-mile radius. Brightview has "good relations with the competition. Another facility [also in Staunton] has only assisted living and memory care, so the sales director there may say, 'I think independent living, like at Brightview, would be better for you.'"

In her 17 years at Brightview, Bradley has interacted with hundreds of families; even asking the names of their pets, since dogs and cats are acceptable for residents. "I love what I do," she concludes. Costs at Brightview's independent living section start at $2,145 per month with dinner and continental breakfast; assisted living, with three meals, costs $4,081 a month.

According to Argentum (2020), Brookdale Senior Living, with assisted living units in 41 states, was ranked as the largest U.S. assisted living provider. One Brookdale sales manager, who travels to two of the company's properties about 30 minutes apart, has worked in sales of all types for about 25 years (personal communication, anonymous, June 16, 2022).

Although only two prospective clients arrived for a Q&A plus food event, a current resident was on hand for a tour of the facility. The sales manager said a district manager visits the location—one of more than 650 in the United States—once a month. Because of its size, Brookdale can create customized gifts for prospective residents, such as a folder containing seven low-or no-sodium spice packets—created, according to the folder's text, "to counteract the loss of taste that is a natural part of the aging process."

Another large U.S. chain of nursing homes, Life Care Centers of America, with 200 facilities in 28 states, pulls in $10 billion in annual revenue (Ariella, 2021). Monthly costs at another type of facility, CCRCs, roughly match those at independent/assisted living chains.

Continuing Care Retirement Communities (CCRCs)

In contrast with independent/assisted living venues, about 80% of the approximately 2,000 U.S. Continuing Care Retirement Communities (CCRCs) are not for profit (Breeding, 2018b; Nelson, 2018), so the communication/marketing staff have somewhat different functions. However, they still need one or more professionals to reach out to prospective new residents, given that death is a fact of CCRC life, as well as to other external and internal publics.

Also in contrast to assisted living venues, CCRCs' levels of care include on-site skilled nursing units; a resident of a venue like Brightview, for example, would need to stay at a rehab setting after surgery. A third contrast involves the fee structure; a CCRC requires a large upfront fee ranging from about $300,000 to $600,000.

Continuing Care Retirement Communities are one option for those who do not choose to or cannot live with family members as they age. CCRCs provide lifestyle amenities like concerts, lectures, fitness classes and art studios, not just health care facilities and meals. Many have religious affiliations, but none has a religion test for admission. Given income disparities, CCRCs' high costs inevitably affect the racial diversity of CCRCs.

THE VILLAGE AT PENN STATE

Madison Glover, a Penn State December 2020 graduate, started working at The Village at Penn State, a CCRC, in February of 2021. Having majored in business with a health sciences minor, she feels she found the perfect first job. Glover and Alanna Parsons, who has worked at The Village for eight years, comprise the sales and marketing staff at this 214-resident CCRC.

"Alanna does everything pre-deposit. I do the post-deposit work," explained Glover (personal communication, July 23, 2021). "Deposit" refers to the large entry payment, which could total many thousands of dollars, that assures an individual or a couple plans to move to the CCRC. The Village had more vacancies than usual in 2021 due to COVID, which made personal visits and move-ins difficult. The Village at Penn State belongs to the Pennsylvania-based Liberty Lutheran group that "impacts the health and well-being of more than 10,000 senior adults" (The Village at Penn State, n.d.).

Alanna Parsons noted that a team at the Philadelphia headquarters coordinated responses for the five CCRCs in her Liberty Lutheran group during COVID (personal communication, February 24, 2021). Parsons and Glover work with two teams of residents: Village Marketing Ambassadors, who meet with prospective residents, and the Reaching Out Committee, who meet with new residents. Linda Morrow, a 16-year resident who volunteers with the newcomers' transition group, explained that she gets a call from marketing "so we can work with newcomers as soon as they are approved," that is, when they have met the medical and financial criteria (personal communication, July 23, 2021). Morrow assigns a welcome host to each newcomer.

Ambassadors, who meet once a month, work with Parsons to meet with prospective residents. They show these prospects their own and others' apartments, answer questions and eat together in the dining hall. A recent larger-scale marketing event involved 15 people who toured a number of apartments, nibbling snacks at each stop.

The Village ranks as a smaller CCRC, with its 156 living units and 36 skilled nursing units. A recent report revealed the following median numbers for CCRCs: independent living units, 120; assisted living units, 43; and skilled nursing units, 72 (Nelson, 2018). Given these three levels of care, usually all on one campus, residents can move from one level to another as their needs change.

U.S. CCRCs

The Village is located in the state having the most CCRCs, Pennsylvania, just under 200 (Nelson, 2018). That state's CCRCs serve mainly seniors who already live there, not new residents of the state. The top three states with more people 60 and over (Horan, 2021) moving in versus out in 2019, make for a robust "senior economy":

1. Florida, net in-migration: 67,093
2. Arizona, net in-migration: 28,060
3. North Carolina, net in-migration: 19,696

In Raleigh, NC, Tom Akins serves as president and CEO of an industry/advocacy group representing 69 CCRCs. These North Carolina members comprise 15,000 staff and 20,000-plus residents. There are 75 business partners. By 2034, the total CCRC economic impact in North Carolina is projected to be $3.2 billion (Appold, Johnson & Parnell, 2015).

Akins and two staff members perform communication functions as well as their other duties. Akins, who came to Raleigh 11 years ago, had worked since 1999 as CEO of a CCRC in Kansas. Trained in public administration, he had earlier worked for a congressman in Kansas, gaining legislative experience. In 2006, national LeadingAge (see below) started a leadership academy, "for which I was in the first class. When this job opened up, I was told that there's not a better place than North Carolina" (personal communication, June 14, 2021). In 2021, Akins worked against a legislative issue, a sales tax on CCRC fees, for which the "cost would be huge. CCRC people are planners. Tax issues would be major"—a disincentive for retirees moving to the state.

"Communication is important," Akins emphasized. One communication function, website design and updating, is handled on a contract basis, using association management software. "In 10 years, that is the first one. It took three evenings with much help from my wife, who worked at a CCRC in Raleigh, to design it. We stole the format from [another organization]. We follow the CASE principle—Copy and Steal Everything."

In relating to member CCRCs, Akins's office works closely with NorC-CRA—the 5,000-member North Carolina Continuing Care Residents Association—that meets two or three times a year. The office devises and presents a 72-month work plan: "Here are some things [to consider]." The office also makes suggestions: Many CCRCs "have book discussion groups. We say, 'Here are some Diversity/Equity/Inclusion ideas' (for books)." Members, along with vendors, attend the LeadingAge annual meeting, planning for which falls to the vice president. In 2021, after a one-year COVID hiatus, "We sold out the hotel room block the first day. People want to be together."

Interestingly, Akins does not place a high priority on media relations, but has still made his mark, both locally (an ABC news story on seniors' voting during COVID) and nationally (in 2018 on NPR for seven minutes after Hurricane Florence). Sometimes the office responds when *NC Health News* sends out an email blast.

Akins believes that it doesn't matter if they are not high profile. "It's hard to start and then stop with the media. If you respond, they call you back. It all takes time! They may [confront you with issues like], 'Why are nursing homes killing all those people?' Our absence from that discussion is not noticeable."

A main communication activity involves speaking to various groups around the state, including boards of directors of member CCRCs—especially about trend analyses. "Here are things you should look at in three to five years. For example, you need to look at technology infrastructure and [its] security. A hack is the last thing a CCRC needs!" To underscore that point, Akins cited a survey of prospective CCRC residents' most-desired amenities; food, which used to rank first, has fallen to last place. Number 1 was internet speed.

LeadingAge: Industry Group

LEADINGAGE, NATIONAL

LeadingAge, an industry group, represents nursing homes, assisted living communities, CCRCs and community organizations. Headquartered in Washington, D.C., to facilitate its lobbying/ advocacy efforts, it aims to be "the trusted voice for aging"; as a 501(c)(3) charity, it focuses on education, advocacy and applied research. Sounding like the phrase "leading edge," the group—formerly called the American Association of Homes and Services for Aging—went through a reorganization, during which a branding firm suggested a name change. The organization works with 38 auxiliary associations, most located in state capitals; some encompass regions rather than states, such as LeadingAge/ Gulf States (LeadingAge, n.d.).

Lisa Sanders, director of media relations for LeadingAge, is one of 86 staff members at the national headquarters. She noted that participation by members in their online webinars on COVID was exceptionally high (personal communication, March 15, 2021). A former journalist (for *Advertising Age, Crain's New York Business, Business Week* and *Forbes*), Sanders joined the national staff in 2017, where she writes as well as pitches story ideas. Previously she ran her own public relations firm for eight and a half years.

Sanders works with Deborah Dailey, communications and media relations manager, who directs email strategy, content creation, scheduling and analytics. Susan Donley, former publisher of Next Avenue, the PBS website for people over 50, serves as senior vice president, marketing and communications.

Sanders, for example, helped Tom Akins in Raleigh, NC, with his NPR story about Hurricane Florence. During COVID, headquarters offered proactive communication assistance to nursing homes and CCRCs. They produced webinars, articles, chats and even copy-and-paste news releases in addition to a complete tool kit for aging service providers to use regarding the pandemic. (See Appendix A).

LEADINGAGE, STATE LEVEL

In Florida, the LeadingAge headquarters in Tallahassee serves four tiers of facilities for seniors: nursing homes, CCRCs, assisted living venues and affordable housing. Its in-house staff of 12 to14 (plus an additional 30 contract persons such as photographers) includes one person specifically dedicated to communication; indeed, Nick Van Der Linden holds the title director of communications.

Earning both an undergraduate and master's in communication from Auburn University in eastern Alabama, he worked at an entry level job in the Florida Department of Health as a public information officer during the Governor Rick Scott administrations. Van Der Linden's duties included handling press releases and general information "until Ebola hit; then a staff change vaulted me into the press secretary post, a 24/7 high-stress job" (personal communication, June 3, 2021). The Department of Health "gets the most media inquiries; it is huge, dealing with many health aspects"—such as water-quality issues related to the Red Tide crisis and emergency preparedness related to Category 5 Hurricane Michael, both in 2018.

Then in 2019, the changeover to Governor Ron DeSantis inevitably meant turnover. Seeing the handwriting on the wall, Van Der Linden in February 2019 joined LeadingAge, enjoying one normal year before COVID hit. (See chapter

3). Media relations constitutes a "major change between my two jobs; at the Department of Health, we had [inquiries] 10 times a day. Now the amount is less, but the nature is the same. We establish relations with reporters. As an association, you want them to tell [our] story. My goal is to increase the brand."

Events, such as the annual August conference, involve various staff persons. Van Der Linden assists another staffer in terms of "any communication about the event." For press conferences about that event or any other event, he works with the CEO, "briefing him, stressing talking points; I make sure my teams . . . photographers . . . are where they should be. What will be asked? You want your message to get out—that's media advocacy."

The job in relation to members involves webinars, emails, video/ audio messages and social media. Pillars of the association are advocacy, education, communication/networking. "We answer queries our members don't know they have," he summarized.

"Every CCRC has a marketing office; many also have a dedicated PR/comm person as well, such as Westminster, which is a large CCRC. The marketing person often serves in the communication role. Affordable housing members don't have that kind of staff. Big nursing homes have staff [that serve that function]. Those that [need comm functions] rely on me and my contract staff. We have a state-wide perspective. In the case of a local government [issue, I say] please work with this local rep."

The Florida group got a grant for therapeutic gardening in nursing homes that resulted in a *McKnight's Long-Term Care News* article. For local happenings, if a "nursing home will have a kick-off event [of some type], I develop materials for them to share with local media."

Relations with national LeadingAge can involve Lisa Sanders or Susan Donley sending out press releases, but because specifics vary from state to state, "We must take care; [that said, the state entities] use each other as resources." National often sends out a weekly "ask" whereby they need local input, such as one in 2021 about federal dollars for affordable housing, which can be used when National does a press conference; "We need names, faces and stories" was their request.

Van Der Linden's typical day starts with a review/monitoring of the news, especially political news of Florida: "Are there fires to put out? Is there a slow story down the road?" He then checks in with his CEO. Every Friday, the office produces a newsletter. They then may work on the annual report, do promos for events or work on the next convention. "You must be flexible and shift gears if a member [needs you]. My priorities have changed three times just today!"

The Florida office publishes a biannual magazine with a sizable readership. However, when one thinks of publications for seniors, one national periodical dwarfs all others. In fact, *AARP The Magazine* dwarfs *all* magazines, bar none.

AARP

Superlatives come naturally to AARP, an influential entity that boasts 38 million members (AARP, n.d.a). Its bimonthly magazine, with a readership of 37 million (*AARP The Magazine*, n.d.) ranks as the largest publication in the world. AARP was named twice by *Fortune* as the most powerful interest group in Washington, D.C., in both 1997 and 1998, after *Fortune* surveyed Capitol Hill staff workers (McAllister, 1998).

AARP "has been a major lobbying force on issues affecting senior citizens such as Social Security and Medicare," but it "allows individuals as young as 50 to join its ranks" (McAllister, 1998). Thus in 1999, the interest group changed its name from the American Association of Retired Persons to its four-letter acronym, since "almost one-third of our members are still working," according to spokeswoman Lisa Davis (McAllister, 1998). AARP focuses on those aged over 50, but persons of all ages may join (for $12 a year for the first year).

AARP has offices in every state, Puerto Rico and the U.S. Virgin Islands, whose staffs are direct employees of national AARP. Chapters within each state are independently run by volunteers who pursue activities such as blood drives and Christmas toy collections.

The Virginia office, located in Richmond, has a strong connection to the national headquarters in the person of that state's director, Jim Dau, who used to work in former senior vice president Jason Young's national external relations department. Young was "navigating a lot of issues. Congress is today dealing with family caregiver legislation and [possible] Medicare and Medicaid cuts. There is a good amount of attention to voter education campaigns and community outreach. We practice offense and defense. What we pursue is a function of triage, based on urgency and importance. We're busy and very big," explains Dau (personal communication, June 29, 2021).

"Big" arguably understates the case when considering AARP's advertising muscle, since the 50-plus U.S. demographic "accounts for more than 53% of all consumer spending" (AARP, n.d.b). AARP publishes three editions of its bimonthly *AARP The Magazine* (formerly *Modern Maturity*), including 50–59, 60–69 and 70+ editions. Advertisers can choose among these three "seamlessly edited age versions" (*AARP The Magazine*, n.d.), wherein the editorial content changes depending the age-specific edition in which it appears; for example, an article on health in the 60–69 edition deals with health matters for that age group.

The 60–69 edition has an audience of 12.144 million, 59% of them female; 69% have a college education, with a median household income of $75,845. The 70+ edition has the highest audience number at 13.296 million, 60% of them female; 65% have a college education, with a median household income of $60,296. (*AARP The Magazine*, n.d.).

AARP The Magazine has a sister publication, the newsprint *AARP Bulletin*, which appears monthly (except February and August). Both are available online.

AARP has an estimated 1,272 employees (Owler, n.d). The communication function alone comprises many positions, depending on how one defines the sector, as well as a number of internships. In fact, multiple ads for SilverComm jobs at the Washington, D.C., headquarters alone were listed in September 2021.

AARP's executive vice president and chief communications/ marketing officer, Martha Boudreau, who earns a salary of $651,679 (Nonprofit Explorer, n.d.), has a high-profile background in public relations. She worked as general manager for FleishmanHillard's Washington, D.C., office. Also with that well-known public relations firm, she served as president for the Mid-Atlantic and Latin American region. FleishmanHillard ranks as the top public relations trainer for the U.S. government, such as working with embassy personnel prior to their assignments at the Davos, Switzerland, economic conference.

"Outdated attitudes about aging are being replaced by the realization that people often live their best lives after 50," Boudreau states. However, she cites "inconsistent access to quality health care and persistent age discrimination in the workplace" as negative realities (AARP, 2021a).

One gets the feeling through reading AARP publications and online material that the 50–65 cohort looms somewhat larger in AARP's priorities than the older old, aged 65 and above, the focus of this book. Typical articles in *AARP The Magazine* feature celebrities who invoke in the reader this reaction: "Wow, I didn't realize s/he has turned 50. S/he looks great!" Moreover, the periodic emails from Shari Horowitz, New York-based associate director, marketing events and promotions, feature five personalities who would soon turn 50. Amy Poehler, for example, hit that major milestone on September 16, 2021; Ben Affleck, on August 15, 2022.

In Retrospect

A question emerges that readers may have been asking themselves throughout this chapter: How does a SilverComm professional deal with the constancy of death? By definition, those whose work life revolves around people in the 60s, 70s, 80s and beyond will experience loss. Gretchen Likins, the director of admissions and public relations for the 500-resident Carol Woods retirement community in Chapel Hill, NC, has reflections on this question, as almost every issue of the community's weekly newsletter has announcements of one or more memorial service; in 2021, 36 residents died (*Carol Woods News*, 2022).

"There is joy in helping others," Likins says (personal communication, March 23, 2022). "People are taken care of so well here. They live full lives. In fact, they live longer when they're here. We have rehab for pain management so residents can walk to the dining room and socialize. I have changed my mindset, as I myself get older. I now truly appreciate older adults and their wisdom." Heather Maurer of Ohio's Hospice (see Box 2.1) must also cope with this reality.

"When I hear a sad story, I think of our mission. Our mission is to celebrate the lives of those we have the privilege of serving," Maurer related. "I also try to

Box 2.1. Communications Practitioner: Ohio's Hospice

Nationally, those 65 and over accounted for more than 70% of hospice patients in 2019 (Michas, 2022), with cancer the largest diagnostic category of a life-limiting condition. In one state, Ohio, the average daily census of patients being served is 1,700-plus. "We serve patients and families in their homes, extended care and assisted living facilities, Hospice Houses and inpatient care centers," stated Heather Maurer (personal communication, June 20, 2022).

Maurer, an Ohio University journalism graduate, worked in newspapers, corporate and marketing communications, university communications and not-for-profit communications before assuming her current position as content team leader for the communications team of Ohio's Hospice, headquarter in Dayton, Ohio.

"I work on a variety of projects including newsletters; media releases; content for marketing collateral such as flyers, rack cards and brochures; media releases; social media; website articles; intranet articles; strategic content and communications planning; event promotion; and any other communications collateral that supports the mission of the organization. I work on both external and internal communications pieces," she explained. Her content team works with a group of graphic designers.

"There is one patient story that stands out to me," recalled Maurer. "I was asked to write about a mother who was dying from cancer. Her daughter's wedding was scheduled for later that summer. As the mother's condition worsened, she expressed regret that she would not live long enough to see her daughter's wedding. The staff at Ohio's Hospice LifeCare, an affiliate of Ohio's Hospice in Wooster, Ohio, helped plan the wedding. I had the honor and privilege of talking with the mother's husband and with the daughter. I felt sad for the family yet honored to share their story on our website."

Event planning has a content component, such as the opening of the new 31,180-square foot Hospice House at Ohio's Hospice in Troy, Ohio, for which Maurer's team "helped plan the communications for the ribbon-cutting event. The Hospice House serves patients who require a higher level of care than they can receive at home."

place myself in the shoes of the family members. I treat others as I would want to be treated. I truly believe that this is the one place I have worked where the staff members really understand the mission of the organization and its values."

In a more practical vein, what other threads pervade the preceding pages? Selling of physical spaces constitutes one—whether spaces in nursing homes like Hickory Creek in Ohio, assisted living units at Brightview in Virginia or independent-living housing at The Village at Penn State. Selling of goods and services, such as via advertisements in *AARP The Magazine* or insurance via direct mail to AARP members, makes for another thread (see Box 2.2).

Selling or promoting ideas constitutes still another thread, such as the advocacy practiced by LeadingAge and AARP. These public relations efforts often involve persuasion at the state and national levels to encourage legislators to adopt policies that do not adversely affect senior citizens. Such efforts fall under what Heath (2013) calls his public relations Persuasion Model, which he explains as an organization's influence on target groups to accept a particular view on certain issues. (An in-depth discussion of persuasion, which has engendered abundant research, [e.g., O'Keefe, 2015], lies beyond the scope of this chapter.)

All the SilverComm professionals interviewed for this chapter deal in some way with customers: for Matthew King, individuals or their families who need 24-hour nursing care; for Michelle Bradley and Angie Via, people who want a safe place to live with meals and activities provided; for Tom Akins, the CCRC members who belong to LeadingAge-North Carolina.

Since these customers have choices, another commonality evident in the preceding pages is competition. Marketing professionals can emphasize elements

Box 2.2.   AARP Mailings and Marketing Materials

The first author, a member of AARP, received the following mailings during one fiscal year—July 1, 2021–June 30, 2022. The first two entries represent marketing of for-profit firms that have a relationship with AARP.

AARP Auto Insurance Program from The Hartford (Hartford, CT): 12 solicitations
AARP Life Insurance Program from New York Life Insurance Company (Tampa, FL): 12 solicitations
AARP Bulletin (newsprint publication), monthly except for 2 double issues: 10 issues
AARP The Magazine (bimonthly slick-paper publication): 6 issues
AARP Benefit Guide: 1 copy
Other (petitions, health-related, AARP Foundation information, etc.): 11 items

such as service, affordability, food quality and internet performance to rise above the competition. While geography can be a deciding factor, competition exists even within a locality. (Unlike those 67,000-plus seniors who relocated to Florida in 2019, most moving takes place locally.)

Events and publications, which help an organization rise above the competition, can range widely. Whether a golf tournament in Ohio, a pie give-away in Virginia or publication of either the largest magazine in the world (AARP) or a limited weekly newsletter (LeadingAge-Florida), all professionals in this chapter carry out activities that fall under the rubric of support planning (Ferguson, 2015).

Still another commonality, especially in the selling of residential space, is the instinctive reliance on source credibility, such as articulated by Hovland and Weiss's (1951) classic research. Both the Village and Brightview enlist residents who, without the sales people present, talk to prospective customers. As Angie Via of Brightview stated, "It's good to hear from a peer, not from Michelle or me."

In sum, "marketing and community relations must be seen as a priority of top management. They cannot pass it all off to subordinates or outside contractors, no matter how good those others may be" (Chies, 2022, p. 456). The SilverComm professionals featured in this chapter would agree. Through their insights, the preceding pages have conveyed the contradiction to the stereotype of doddering elders. Not one interviewee used the word "depressing."

Chapter 2. Projects and Exercises

1. Interview professionals at a local AARP or LeadingAge chapter. What is their typical day like? What path led them to their current position?
2. Interview marketing directors at a local assisted living venue that belongs to a chain, such as the Brightview, Brookdale or Life Care Centers groups.
3. Watch *Some Kind of Heaven*, a 2021 documentary about a Florida community where 130,000 retirees live. Write a review of the documentary.
4. Visit AARP's website (https://www.aarp.org/) and peruse what the website offers. Suggest some ideas of how to make the website better for the target audience.
5. Find a nursing home in or near your hometown that has a social media platform. Interview the person(s) responsible about strategies used on the platform.

CHAPTER 3

Practitioners' COVID Year

Coauthored with Bojinka Bishop, associate professor emerita, Ohio University

Lucia DeClerck, a resident of Mystic Meadows Rehab and Nursing in Egg Harbor, New Jersey, tested positive for COVID-19 on January 25, 2021—her 105th birthday. Happily, she garnered headlines when she recovered (Tully, 2021). However, DeClerck's upbeat story contrasts with sobering facts about the vulnerability of elder residents in retirement homes. In the United States, 95% of U.S. COVID deaths have been among adults 50 and older (AARP, 2020).

Given that the risk for contracting COVID increases steadily as one ages, facilities where many senior citizens live in close quarters pose elevated risks regarding the virus (Applegate & Ouslander, 2020). As of November 24, 2020, reported deaths of residents and staff in nursing homes passed the 100,000 mark—likely an undercount (Chidambaram, Garfield & Neuman, 2020). Not until April of 2020 did the Centers for Medicaid and Medicare require nursing homes to report COVID cases to the Center for Disease Control and Prevention.

The Kaiser Family Foundation points to the difficulty of knowing exactly how many elders in what kind of living-in facility had COVID. In six states, deaths in long-term care facilities account for more than half of all COVID deaths (Chidambaram, 2020). With 1.3 million people residing in nursing homes, they get the lion's share of attention, but other types of facilities for older Americans exist, such as assisted living venues with 800,000 residents and Continuing Care Retirement Communities (CCRCs) with about 600,000 residents.

CCRCs, where residences can range from studio apartments to luxury villas, offer all three basic need levels for seniors: independent living, assisted living and skilled nursing. A Mather LifeWays Institute on Aging study of 5,000 seniors living in 80 U.S. CCRCs found residents enjoying healthier, happier lives than non-CCRC seniors (Breeding, 2018a). If this good health has persisted during COVID, what practices have contributed to that positive outcome?

Table 3.1. Continuing Care Retirement Communities: Interviewees, Employers, Metrics

	# Mktg/PR Staff	# Residents	Average Age
1. Anonymous Durham, NC / Protestant Marketing director, 24 years*	5	675	declined to say
2. The Village at Penn State, 260 Lions Hill Road State College, PA 16803/ Lutheran Retireatpennstate .org Alanna Parsons Director of sales, 8 years*	2	214	82
3. Kendal at Oberlin, 600 Kendal Drive, Oberlin, OH 44074/ Quaker Kao.kendal.org Maggie Dohn Stark Director of marketing and admission, 27 years*	4	350	82/83
4. Anonymous Suburban Kansas City, KS/ Protestant Director of marketing and sales, 2 months*	6	700	declined to say
5. Frasier Retirement Community, 350 Ponca Place Boulder, CO 80303/ Methodist Frasiermeadows.org Julie Soltis Director of communication, 6 years*	4	476	82
6. The Village at Mary's Woods, 17520 Mesnard St Oswego, OR97034/ Catholic Villageatmaryswoods.org Cheri Mussotto-Conyers Vice president, marketing and communication, 16 years*	7	750	81

Note: Listed east to west. Affiliation may be historical rather than denominational; all are non-profit.
* indicates length of time with current employer

What role did communication play? One sector of a typical CCRC staff is a communication/marketing person or persons.

This chapter presents original, unpublished research on the experiences, lessons learned and measures for coping employed by SilverComm professionals at six CCRCs in six U.S. states. (See Table 3.1). The practitioners, confronted with a pandemic that especially threatened the elderly, dealt not with a quick-onset crisis like an earthquake, but a pandemic that evolved in stages. Having lasted about a year at the time of the interviews with practitioners, COVID did not at first have a clear end point—in other words, it was a lingering crisis. Their work addressed various stakeholders: residents, staff, families of residents, prospective residents and communities within which the facilities were located.

COVID and the Profession

Information on how to communicate about COVID was a constant topic in the trade and professional world after the U.S. declaration of a public health emergency February 3, 2020. The CDC, CMS and state health departments all specified certain rules for communicating about COVID precautions and cases. In addition, professional, trade and lobbying groups provided guidance on communication. Still, practitioners had to address situations particular to their organizations, such as a senior-travel nonprofit that had to stop all its tours. (See Box 3.1).

A review of The Public Relations Society of America website (March 2021) showed that the society held at least 12 webinars on COVID and crisis response between March 2020 and March 2021, in addition to at least a dozen articles on communicating about COVID. Ragan, a major trade publisher for the communication profession, published articles and hosted webinars each week on COVID communication (as evidenced by emails received by one of the authors). *PR Week*, another trade publication, in partnership with Haymarket Media also published articles and hosted webinars every week on COVID communication and response (also based on emails received by chapter coauthor Bojinka Bishop).

LeadingAge, an industry group which represents more than 5,000 aging service providers (see chapter 2) offered proactive communication assistance to nursing homes and CCRCs. They produced webinars, articles, chats and even copy-and-paste news releases (see Appendix A), in addition to a complete tool kit for aging service providers to use regarding the pandemic. Lisa Sanders, director of media relations for LeadingAge, noted that participation by members in their online webinars on COVID was exceptionally high (personal communication, March 15, 2021).

Box 3.1. How Did Road Scholar (Formerly Elderhostel) Survive COVID?

When President Trump declared COVID a national emergency and put COVID travel restrictions into effect on March 13, 2020, travel for Americans came to an immediate halt. And educational travel for seniors was a particularly challenging field to be in. "With hundreds of thousands of our participants now isolated (many of them alone) in their homes, we knew that—as a not-for-profit—we needed to find another way to pursue our mission of lifelong learning. So we immediately got to work on creating a virtual campus," said Kelsey Knoedler Perri, PR director at Road Scholar and a member of the team who developed Road Scholar's first Virtual Lecture Series.

By March 26, 2020, Road Scholar launched their first one-hour Virtual Lecture. After a successful spring series, they added multiday Adventures Online to their repertoire. All of Road Scholar's virtual programs take place on Zoom. "They're always live and interactive and feature our renowned expert instructors from all over the world." The one-hour Virtual Lectures use Zoom webinar, and viewers are invited to type questions live using the "question and answer" function at the end of the session. Road Scholar's multiday Adventures Online aim to recreate the in-person educational travel experience as much as possible. They use Zoom meeting, so all participants are on camera, and include live lectures and performances, interactive discussions, virtual field trips and more. "The social connections participants make on our in-person programs are such an important part of the Road Scholar experience, so we needed to make sure that was an element of our online programming as well," said Perri. "We have seen what a lifeline these programs have been for our participants and have committed to making virtual programming a permanent part of Road Scholar's offerings."

Road Scholar also tightened budgets across the entire organization. They significantly reduced marketing efforts, most noticeably halting all print mailings for a period of time, and transitioned to a fully remote working model. And they were forced to make some difficult staffing decisions, cutting hours and benefits and reducing the size of the team. "Since we saw enrollments starting to increase in 2021, taking care of our staff and rehiring has been our first priority," said Perri.

Road Scholar is a not-for-profit, so in March 2020, they launched a multichannel fundraising campaign. Road Scholar resumed a select number of programs in July 2021 and has been adding to their list of offerings since then.

Continuing Care Retirement Communities (CCRCs)

Continuing Care Retirement Communities (CCRCs) are one option for those who do not choose to or cannot live with family members as they age (Ji & Cooper, 2017). CCRCs provide lifestyle amenities like concerts, lectures, fitness classes and art studios, not just health care facilities (Hangley, 2022). Many have religious affiliations. They typically (about two-thirds of U.S. CCRCs) require a large entry fee, followed by a monthly fee (which includes housing and often meals, depending on the plan a resident chooses). Given income disparities, the high costs inevitably affect the racial diversity of CCRCs.

About 80% of the approximately 2,000 U.S. CCRCs are not for profit. A recent report revealed the following median numbers for CCRCs: independent living units, 120; assisted living units, 43; and skilled nursing units, 72 (Nelson, 2018). Given these three levels of care, usually all on one campus, residents can move from one level to another as their needs change.

The same report, prepared by the Ziegler specialty investment bank, found that five states have the most CCRCs: Pennsylvania (in first place, with 200), Ohio, California, Florida and Illinois. Only Wyoming has no CCRCs at all (Nelson, 2018). No matter what their location, they need one or more professionals to reach out to prospective new residents, given that death is a fact of CCRC life, as well as to other external and internal publics. At one CCRC (not in this study), 30 residents died in 2020, or 6% of its resident population, but not from COVID (*Carol Woods News*, 2021). That said, seniors at CCRCs do live longer than the elderly at other care facilities (Breeding, 2018a).

Crisis Communication

An early study of public relations scholarship, 1975–1986 (Pasadeos & Renfro, 1992), used citation analysis; that study marked the emergence of a distinct public relations scholarship (Ha & Riffe, 2015). Within this scholarship, crisis communication has attracted and continues to attract significant attention (e.g., Sellnow & Seeger, 2021). The classic textbook *Crisis Communication* (Fearn-Banks, 2016) is now in its fifth edition.

Much of crisis research is based on situational crisis communication (SCC) theory, regarding the effects of crises on organizational reputation. Coombs (1995, 2009), along with others (e.g., Coombs & Holladay, 1996), holds that, as a result of negative events, stakeholders will attribute blame, which will affect how they relate to the organization. Benoit's (1995) image restoration theory, now revised to image repair theory (Benoit, 1997), proposes that, once damaged, images cannot be completely restored, but can be repaired.

Of relevance to this chapter, Cameron's contingency theory deals with external crises with a high threat level and long duration; he and colleagues (Cancel et al., 1997) offered alternatives to the two-way symmetrical model. Their theory relates to communication between an organization and external publics; the practitioner's effectiveness depends on the circumstances at particular moments in time. Later, Cancel and colleagues (1999) tested variables that affected the continuum from accommodation to advocacy. The theory focuses on a threat's type and duration; those two factors determine the threat level, indicating that external threats like COVID create more demands than internal ones, requiring more resources.

Vincent T. Covello (2003), director of New York's Center for Risk Communication, deals with health issues in setting forth seven best practices to include in a crisis plan. In abbreviated form, they are: (1) involve stakeholders; (2) listen; (3) be truthful; (4) coordinate with credible sources; (5) meet the needs of the media; (6) communicate clearly and compassionately; and (7) plan thoroughly and carefully.

Qualitative approaches are an underexplored direction in crisis communication research. Ha and Riffe (2015) compared crisis communication research published in 27 communication and 42 business journals. Communication journals' crisis research, which focused heavily on the effects of crisis management, used a quantitative approach and content analyses, with media articles as sources. Business journals' crisis research articles used a qualitative approach, with practitioners as sources. To redress the dearth of such research in communication, this chapter will qualitatively focus on practitioners.

Original Research: CCRC Practitioners

Avery et al. (2010) emphasize that the crisis communication field remains open for new directions in context and critique. Thus the present research begins to explore not a bolt-from-the-blue crisis, but an evolving, "creeping" crisis—specifically in the health sector with a focus on older Americans who live in not-for-profit communities. It will use qualitative methodology.

RESEARCH METHOD

Interviewing practitioners lends insights to communication research (Cancel, Mitrook & Cameron, 1999). Communicators and/or marketers (whichever function was responsible for communication) at CCRCs who agreed to be interviewed for this study (see Table 3.1) worked in six states: North Carolina, Pennsylvania, Ohio, Kansas, Colorado and Oregon. Two, in Ohio and Colorado, are among the roster of 216 venues accredited by the Commission on Accreditation of Rehabilitation Facilities (CARF), a small portion of all CCRCs. The other four represent the vast majority of the approximately 2,000 U.S. CCRCs (Nelson, 2018).

The authors developed a questionnaire after many iterations that covered aspects of how practitioners responded to COVID, the scale and severity of which none of these practitioners had ever encountered. After the six agreed to be interviewed, all asked for the questions in advance. The authors conducted the interviews by phone, except for a Zoom call to the Oregon CCRC, which involved two interviewees. The interviews often ranged beyond a strict Q&A format. Transcripts totaled 28 pages, so a wealth of information had to be curtailed and telescoped in this chapter.

Each coauthor conducted interviews with three CCRCs, lasting from 25 minutes to 2.5 hours. (The Colorado CCRC required two interviews to work through the questions, 90 minutes and 60 minutes.) The interviews took place February 17 to March 3, about one year since the U.S. onset of COVID. Two of the CCRC communicators (in North Carolina and Kansas) preferred to answer anonymously.

The authors examined the websites of all six CCRCs to discern what if any COVID information appeared when the website was first opened and that information's prominence. Did a clickable band immediately appear clearly labeled as COVID related? Was it eye-catching, for example, a swath of color?

RESULTS

The authors' 28 pages of transcripts will be telescoped for clarity in the form of six questions. By way of introduction, Table 3.1 shows a consistent average age for practitioners' stakeholder residents: 82. The number of residents ranged from 214 (the Village at Penn State) to 750 (The Village at Mary's Woods in Oregon). The average number of residents was 528.

All six nonprofits have varying degrees of religious affiliations. Methodist roots characterize Frasier in Boulder, Colorado. The Kendal organization of 13 communities in eight states, represented here by Kendal at Oberlin in Ohio, built its first senior venue in 1973 "based on Quaker values" (Kendal, n.d.). The Village at Mary's Woods in Oregon began as a retirement home for nuns in 1910. The Village at Penn State belongs to the Pennsylvania-based Liberty Lutheran group that "impacts the health and well-being of more than 10,000 senior adults" (Liberty Lutheran, 2021). No venue in this study had a faith test for entry.

Q1. How are communication/marketing staffs configured at the six CCRCs in six states included in this study?

Table 3.1 shows a wide range of employment length, from two months to 27 years; indeed, Maggie Stark had planned to retire after 26 years with Kendal at

Oberlin in Ohio, but "a transition at this [COVID] time would have been so hard, so I said I'd stay on [until April 2, 2021]." Several of the six practitioners had experience in other fields, often health related: in pharmaceutical sales and at a hospice agency, a hospital and a state health department. Non-health-field experience included planned-community real estate development. Three of the six earned undergraduate degrees in communication.

Table 3.1 also shows that the CCRC with the fewest residents, 214 (The Village at Penn State) also had the fewest staff members, two people, while the CCRC with the most residents, 750 (The Village at Mary's Woods in Oregon) had the largest staff, seven people. A rough ratio of about one staff member for every 100-plus residents characterized the facilities.

The titles of the six practitioners interviewed give a telling picture of varied yet overlapping responsibilities. The words *marketing, sales* and *communication* characterize all the practitioners except for Maggie Stark, whose work also included admissions (director of marketing and admission). Titles of staff members who report to those six often include the words *associate, assistant, coordinator* and *counselor*. One staff member at the Oregon CCRC, who has the title *brand and social media manager*, did all internal branding, design and production. Some CCRCs have staff members who coordinate move-in services for new residents or who have the title *client relations*, all under the aegis of the marketing section.

Q2. What is the gender of communication practitioners at the six CCRCs in six states included in this study?

All six of the practitioners are female. As far as the authors could tell, all the staff people who report to those practitioners are also female. This assumption grew from mentions of names during the six interviews (e.g., "Elizabeth is the assistant director of sales") or use of pronouns like "she."

Q3. If COVID cases occurred at any of the six CCRCs in this study, how did practitioners deal with that occurrence?

All six practitioners had to deal with communicating about actual cases (both staff and residents). Fortunately, none reported any deaths directly from COVID. As required by official directives, notifications of positive tests had to be reported; these went out by emails, internal TV stations, newsletters, daily paper copies and notifications on the COVID FAQ section of the CCRC's website. One said that her state's department of health "is a part of [my] life now. All positives [cases] have to be reported. We would put that fact in the newsletter and that the resident is in quarantine, but we couldn't say who.

Contact tracing [involves saying], 'You may have been exposed,' but HIPAA [Health Insurance Portability and Accountability Act] means we could not say by whom." Another practitioner said COVID affected only one resident, who came back from the hospital with a mild case. Several stressed the importance of immediate responses.

Q4. How did practitioners deploy COVID information on the six CCRCs' websites?

All six used websites to reach external publics, which could include families of residents as well as prospective residents and the mass media, but which internal publics could also access.

The authors' March 12–15 content analysis of the six CCRCs' website landing pages revealed that only one (Anonymous) had no mention of COVID; the marketing director said that assisted living and skilled nursing, "We're not required by CMS to post website information."

The other anonymous CCRC's landing page featured a dark red banner across the top, "COVID-19 Update: XXX residents are included as first priority for COVID-19 Vaccine. Learn more today [a live link] or visit the LCS website [live link] for ongoing updates." That link took one to the website of a national CCRC management service.

For Frasier Retirement Community, at the top of the landing page in the dropdown bar one saw "Covid Updates," with links to more detailed information, such as video messages and two newsletters, *C-Updates*, and *Keepin' Busy Bulletin*. The "Covid Updates" also included such information as which vaccine was administered to staff, contractors and residents; when; and what percent of employees, contractors and residents received it (high 91% to 100% for all categories).

The most prominent feature of the Village at Penn State's website was a dark blue band across its top, with two choices for click-through information, plus an X to close out the band. The CDC link had a lead story titled "When You've Been Fully Vaccinated" and a menu for further information. The Pennsylvania Department of Health gave state-specific information. At the bottom of the page, a clickable link specific to the Village led one to 16 FAQs, such as "Does The Village have any positive residents?" A three-sentence answer begins, "At this time, The Village does not have any positive cases."

Kendal at Oberlin likewise featured a dark "COVID-19 Updates" band at the top of its website, also with a close out X. If one did click through, the information was specific to Kendal, beginning with a story titled, "Kendal at Oberlin's Focus is Calm Preparedness." The story encouraged stakeholders to "visit this page often for the most recent information." A further link detailed "why Kendal is one of the Safest Places You Can Be."

On the Village at Mary's Woods website, one saw a prominent green strip across the bottom that read, "How Mary's Woods is responding to Covid-19." On March 15, 2020, a recent update (March 12) popped up when one clicked the "Learn more!" link. The story, which stated that 89.4% of the campus is fully or partially vaccinated, went on to say that the CCRC's "first round of clinics in January/February were the largest on-site clinics CVS Pharmacy had administered in Oregon"—more than 400 (health staff and health unit residents) getting both Pfizer shots. With 95% of independent living residents getting their shots on or off the grounds, "restricted visitation" could now resume.

Q5. Regarding internal publics (CCRC residents), what technology challenges emerged in CCRC communication?

Several practitioners mentioned internal TV systems that all residents have access to, but COVID increased the use of such systems (such as with daily COVID broadcasts) or was the catalyst for adding more channels. At Kendal at Oberlin, "Levels differ; those in their 60s versus those in their 90s. Those in the care center are older and frailer," said Maggie Stark. "Our I.T. Department—a lot of work for them—helped set things up, and the residents' association has a technical committee with people with expertise." The Village at Mary's Woods in Oregon "gave everyone iPads, but not everyone is comfortable with that technology," agreed Cheri Mussotto-Conyers. "Families have access to portals. We added to the website regularly."

One anonymous practitioner mentioned direct telephone calls and posted signage, while another noted that "every family member gets an email on Friday with COVID updates." Julie Soltis of Frasier in Boulder noted increased reliance on newsletters, which were hand-delivered to the door of each resident, whereas "before COVID, we would just have them available in the mail rooms in the buildings." At the Village at Penn State, "We have a list of residents who want hard copies, which go to their in-house mailboxes. All communication throughout the pandemic is sent out to residents via email, which most residents prefer."

In terms of technology, the preference for email mentioned by some practitioners is borne out by corporate experience. A survey of 264 corporate communicators affirmed its primacy, as the "asynchronous nature of email makes it the perfect tool" (DesRochers, 2021).

Q6. What non-technological approaches were used to deal with COVID-related communication?

Under the new normal, practitioners' workloads shot up exponentially. In the words of Alanna Parsons of the Village at Penn State, "We saw [early on] a drastic increase in communication." Maggie Stark of Ohio concurred: "Communication is much different; it's five days a week." In addition to implementing new technologies (see Q5), in order to prevent the virus's spread, practitioners had to publicize the need to wash hands and mask up, conform to CDC and state COVID case reporting rules, inform residents of dining closures and options, explain visitation rules, cancel events, help deliver exercise classes online and eventually help medical personnel organize vaccinations. Long before vaccine availability, however, teams were formed.

"The minute we read about COVID on a Friday, we met on Saturday morning," said Cheri Mussotto-Conyers of Mary's Woods in Oregon. "Our group met at first daily, then morphed into meeting weekly." That team included "key players—health services, clinical staff, care center [skilled nursing] staff. The team members all have [dedicated] staff portals." At Kendal in Ohio, Maggie Stark called the New Normal Committee, composed of staff and residents, "Phenomenal!"

The administrative team at the anonymous North Carolina CCRC "was on top of everything on day one—March 12, 2020." Alanna Parsons of the Village at Penn State noted that a team in Philadelphia coordinated responses for the five CCRCs in her Liberty Lutheran group. Frasier in Colorado called its group a Command Center, which operated 24 hours a day until vaccines were available.

Frasier's Julie Soltis also created other innovations: "In the summer [of 2020] we were able to open up some visiting pods with Plexiglas; we called them Love Pods." Similarly, in February of 2021, Kendal in Ohio "formed [optional] bubbles two weeks after the last vaccination, six people at a time, in residents' cottages. This is a concept from New Zealand, which [greatly helped] very lonely people, especially single people," said Maggie Stark.

The CCRCs' immediate communities constituted another external public to which practitioners related during COVID. They pointed to mostly positive and some negative aspects of their locations. Three of the six were near higher education institutions: Kendal of Ohio, near Oberlin College; Frasier, near the University of Colorado–Boulder; and the Village at Penn State, where Alanna Parsons mentioned some prospective residents' hesitancy to visit due to publicity about COVID spikes at Penn State's Greek organizations and student gatherings.

Julie Soltis of Frasier in Boulder mentioned her proactive, positive relation with the local press: "At first people thought we were covered with cases, but we weren't, so I got quotes from our incident commander. When we had outdoor concerts, I would call the press. And we got great press from having our Love Pods."

At Mary's Woods in Lake Oswego, Oregon, the community ties go back to 1859, when 12 Sisters of the Holy Names of Jesus and Mary got off a steamer and established a girls' school in the Northwest Territory. The 1910 Mother House on the CCRC's campus is a local landmark.

DISCUSSION AND CONCLUSIONS

This qualitative analysis of interviews with six practitioners, all female, at six CCRCs in six states revealed a difficult COVID year, which at the outset had no end point. All experienced increased workloads when implementing measures to protect the vulnerable elderly residents at their facility, since 8 of 10 COVID deaths have occurred in the 65-and-over age group. All six had to deal with required and voluntary reporting of actual cases, but none had to deal with deaths of residents from COVID. Websites at five of the six included prominent and updated COVID information. Practitioners had to deal with differing technology comfort levels among the residents, who commonly ranged from iPad and email users to those who preferred paper copies. Difficult, often heartbreaking, situations involved families who could not visit loved ones and isolated residents who missed spirit-lifting meals and events; when activities had to be canceled, the six had to innovate ways to compensate. Working with a team at the CCRC enabled the practitioners to manage throughout an unprecedented year.

External Variables

The study highlighted a Cameron (Cancel et al., 1997) contingency theory *external* variable—a specific external public (potential CCRC residents) and a characteristic of that public (fear). Internal communicator Alanna Parsons of the Village at Penn State noted her dilemma in counteracting people's hesitancy to visit, much less move in, given Penn State's rather high student COVID positivity rate. Parsons posted clear, unequivocal statements on the COVID Q&A section of her CCRC's website.

CCRCs and skilled nursing facilities both belong to the elder care services industry (Freedonia, 2018), but the *external* threat of negative publicity about nursing homes could elicit strong characteristics—anger plus fear—within external publics (potential residents and their families). Since 70% are for profit, nursing homes' up to 50% share of U.S. COVID deaths (Jaffe, 2020) reflects justified bad press, which could affect their bottom lines.

Elasticity and Change

Borrowing a concept from economics, psychologist John Studdon (2017) applied the principle of elasticity to humans' relation to change; if people know very little about something, then an addition to their store of knowledge can cause a major change in their beliefs. Writing about behavior change, McWilliams (2020) states about COVID that we can "view this as an opportunity to rethink the ways we've always done things, and hold space for something possibly better"; for example, there are "possibilities for incorporating technology into traditional in-person formats in the future."

Indeed, the practitioners found that CCRC residents, once change had entered their lives, did not revert back to former ways of doing things; technology stands out as an additive in one sense and a replacement in another. For example, in-person events will not precisely return in their previous formats. An anonymous practitioner in Kansas City stated that she is "almost glad it happened; we won't be limited on parking, and it will be awesome not to be limited on attendance. It took a lot of time to set up all events over Zoom, but [when we go back to normal] we will be virtual; events with speakers will use Zoom." (See chapter 1, Technology section.)

Alanna Parsons of the Village at Penn State concurred: "The digital platforms we have utilized have been very beneficial and will likely continue. There will be less paper communication. Independent living residents will each be given an iPad. It would have been great to have this [access] earlier." An anonymous practitioner in Kansas City said, "When we have a big national speaker—and only have room for 100 people—now we will not be limited; people can tune in by Zoom."

An anonymous practitioner in North Carolina agreed, saying, "Given the familiarization that people are now feeling with Zoom and Facetime, I assume we will continue to give virtual tours, especially to people from out of town." Likewise, Maggie Stark of Kendal at Oberlin cited the permanence of Zoom, including "garage concerts by some of the many musicians who live here," since Oberlin is a conservatory as well as a college.

Julie Soltis of Frasier in Boulder cited COVID as a catalyst: "We talked about doing stuff like this prior to COVID; now we will continue." The staff will be more active in the use of the four dedicated internal TV channels, which are included in the CCRC's cable package. "Before COVID we didn't use them much, but afterward . . . we videotaped wellness, massage and yoga classes. We added movies. Board meetings were on Zoom so folks could come in live. We will continue recording the board meeting." Furthermore, they will continue delivering the newsletter and allowing "our very elevated, full menu" for to-go. "There is always a silver lining," she concluded.

St. Mary's Woods in Oregon has "become much more interactive. We had to stop large group tours but had to continue marketing and selling. So we took photos of every home available [for move in]. Flyover tours were created. Virtual tours will continue. We will engage off site." Moreover, the Wednesday videos that CEO Diane Hood recorded will continue, as will *The Community Insider* newsletter.

The Concept of a Lingering Crisis

Terms like *event* and *occurrence* or a phrase like *a crisis strikes* appear in crisis communication studies. However, in the case of COVID, practitioners had to take a "dealing with it," preventive approach. In early 2020, the pandemic had no visible end, since most vaccines take 10–12 years to develop (Gregerson, 2020). In July 2020, Moderna trials of healthy under-65s; compromised under-65s; and over 65s showed an immune response. On July 27, Pfizer and BioN-Tech partnered with the Department of Health and Human Services and the Defense Department to deliver their vaccine candidate by December if Phase 3 trials succeeded, but that positive outcome was far from certain.

As Tumin and Bogert (2021) stated on the one-year anniversary of the World Health Organization's declaration of a global pandemic, "For many, the beginning of something different was not a single event, but a cascade of decisions." At the one-year point, 533,904 Americans had died. The one-year duration, which changed almost every aspect of CCRC life, finally had begun to ease. Visits to ailing residents in skilled nursing, which had to stop for many months, could now begin to resume. Throughout, CCRCs had to alter how they dealt with death (not from COVID).

"When a death occurred [for example, in a skilled nursing private room]," said Maggie Stark of Kendal in Ohio, "we had to decide, how will the family clear out their relative's room? They had to crawl through the window while the door remained shut" so as to preserve the safety of other patients. (All of Kendal's rooms are on ground floors.)

"We do a postmortem after any crisis," said Cheri Mussotto-Conyers of Mary's Woods in Oregon, "but none of us expected the magnitude of this in our lifetime. [Now we know that] there may be other pandemics in the future."

Fluid Internal/External Communication

Of the practitioners who gave a specific answer regarding the percentage of their staff's work dealing with external communication, one said 80%, one said 75% and one (a director of marketing and sales) said 100%. Interestingly, Julie Soltis of Frasier in Colorado said that, prior to the pandemic, 30% of her work was internal communication, 70% external; during the pandemic that ratio shifted to 80% internal and only 20% external.

Website updates stand out as an example of overlapping internal/external targeting. "The distinction is fluid," said Maggie Stark of Kendal in Ohio. "Internal people [residents and staff] use 'external' media." For example, websites provided updates on COVID for families of residents who would normally visit in person, whereas formerly websites reached mainly external prospective newcomers. Further, families of residents have a fluid internal/external status when they have phone calls and Zoom, but no in-person visits. Which are they? For the time being, they are both.

As David Sanger (2021) wrote in the *New York Times* at the pandemic's one-year point, even the 9/11 tragedy "did not alter day-to-day life" as COVID had; "no country can go through this kind of trauma without being changed forever." Sanger concluded that the first 12 months of COVID "may prove to be one of the most consequential years in American history." Maggie Stark of Kendal in Ohio put it this way: "We are COVID fatigued; it's been quite a year."

Chapter 3. Projects and Exercises

1. Interview the marketing/ public relations/ sales staff at a CCRC or other senior living/ retirement facility near you; how did they deal with COVID?
2. Look up media coverage of COVID's effect on senior living venues in your area during 2020. How much coverage occurred and when? Who was interviewed? (Families of older residents who died? Staff at the facilities? Public health officials?)
3. Analyze the COVID-related webinars that the Public Relations Society of America, Ragan and *PR Week* created in 2021. What topics predominated? How did these topics change over time?
4. Explore a possible connection between COVID and senior citizens' loneliness. How did they cope or not cope with a lack of human contact?
5. Interview senior citizens about learning to use social media platforms during COVID. Ask them about their main motivations. Did isolation spur them to adopt any new digital techniques to communicate with their friends or family members?

Part II

ADVERTISING

CHAPTER 4

Seniors' Portrayals in Mainstream Media Advertising

Anyone who was watching television in 1984 will likely remember the series of 30-second TV spots for Wendy's that featured three older women. One held a magnifying glass that she used to examine a coin-sized burger almost dwarfed by the pickle that sat atop it; another commented or looked on with fascination; a third intoned, in a strong but petulant voice, "Where's the beef?" The four-foot-ten former manicurist, Clara Peller, was in her 80s when the ad propelled her into popular culture stardom because of those three little words.

The campaign, created by the Dancer Fitzgerald Sample agency, proved phenomenally successful for Wendy's. Indeed, Peller helped to raise Wendy's annual revenue by 31%, the fast-food chain said (*New York Times*, 1987). However, an assessment by Ken Dychtwald (2021, p. 8), an AARP analyst of age bias in the media, said of the ad, "What's so funny about insensitivity, caricature and ridicule?" Dychtwald prefers a 1987 McDonald's ad called "The New Kid" that featured a real employee who had joined the fast-food chain as part of a senior hiring program. He points out that those who create ads skew toward the youthful; the median age of managers in U.S. agencies is 37, while that of creative people is 28.

Chuck Nyren (2021, para. 8), a not-youthful advertising practitioner (born about 1950), begs to differ, calling the critique of Clara Peller "overzealous"; he applauds the "perspicacity and bluntness of old age" depicted in the Wendy's series. What do seniors other than Nyren think of their own presence in advertising?

"Most advertisers receive a failing grade in their efforts to understand and relate to older adults," states Chip Conley, founder of the Modern Elder Academy (Dychtwald, 2021, p. 8). A 2021 AARP survey found that nearly half of older citizens saw "outdated stereotypes," while 62% wished for more realistic portrayals. An earlier AARP survey in 2019 found that only 15% of models in online images were over 50 (Dychtwald, 2021),

In a national sample of adults, Shavitt, Lowery and Haefner (1998) found a disconnect between how younger adults (18 to 34) viewed advertisements, compared to older adults (55 to 64), who were more likely to feel offended by them and less likely to enjoy them.

Courting the Older Consumer

In the quest to discover what approaches evoke positive responses among elders (Moschis, 1992), Bradley and Longino (2001, p. 20), who reviewed various research studies, conclude that a focus on "the role of grandparents may be especially effective because it appeals to the core values of social connectedness and autonomy." Using nonspecific core values like those two examples will appeal to the greatest number of senior consumers, they conclude.

In addition to appeals to core values, the visual aspect of ad portrayals affects marketing decisions. Should models in ads be the same age of the targeted seniors or younger? Since healthy, active seniors "perceive themselves to be 75 to 80 percent of their actual chronological age," models should be 10 to 15 years younger than the target audience (Bradley & Longino, 2001, p. 20). However, these authors emphasize that effective choice of models varies with the product. Face cream ads, which relate to self-image (looking one's best), have effectively used younger models. By contrast, ads for wheelchairs or even adult diapers, which relate to issues of growing old, often use silver models.

Many models' agencies have divisions that include senior models; the Silver Agency, established in 2012, represents senior models exclusively. Some full-service agencies, such as Peter Hubbell's BoomAgers, have a clear focus. Hubbell, author of *The Old Rush: Marketing for Gold in the Age of Aging* (2014), has more than 30 years' experience as an ad man. He cites four themes that will affect how one should approach this lucrative market (pp. 126–128):

1. Well-being: Boomers take care of themselves, thus staying active longer than any previous generation.
2. Simplicity and streamlining: Boomers desire to diverge from the complexity of modern life.
3. Growth: aging is change, not decline.
4. Home-centricity: an array of services and products that enhance home life.

In addition to *The Old Rush*, an older handbook, *Advertising to Baby Boomers*, was written by Chuck Nyren (2005, see above). "We appreciate a witty turn of phrase, a humorous slant on things, even slightly skewed personas dramatized or pitching products. Just make sure the wit isn't derogatory, the humor isn't embarrassing, and the personas aren't doddering" (p. 11). He proposes guidelines that should inform Boomer-targeted ads.

1. Design: not overly glossy or busy, with fonts comfortably but not insultingly large.
2. Copy: not overhyped; assume the audience has time to absorb information in a seamless presentation.

Both practitioners' insights (see Box 4.1) and research findings have value in understanding the senior market. Since "advertising functions as a cultural institution" (Yanni, 1990, p. 71), how does that institution depict, or not depict, elders as shown in ads? One researcher states that "advertising can make sense with consumers by tapping into discourses which are already out there in the world" (Hackley, 1999, p. 163). Of course, not everything "out there" is faithfully replicated, since "content does not perfectly describe reality. . . . It singles out and highlights certain elements over others" (Shoemaker & Reese, 1996, p. 37).

Richard Pollay (1986), using the metaphor of the "distorted mirror," posits that advertising highlights only those elements that can persuade consumers to make purchases. With Gallagher, Pollay (1990) analyzed magazine ads 1900–1980 and TV commercials 1970–1980. They concluded that advertising indeed

Box 4.1. Agency Interview: Advertir, Inc.

Advertir, Inc., a full-service agency (direct, digital, and print, among other services) is located in McAllen, Texas. With 40 years of experience, CEO and president Christopher Julian noted the large amount of "health care and pharmaceutical advertising being placed, all using seniors" as models (personal communication, June 8, 2022). Advertir represents the Advantage Medicare plan provider in South Texas; Reno, Nevada; and West Palm Beach, Florida; for that client, "we certainly use 65-plus models," said Julian, a native of Baton Rouge, Louisiana. (See Box 4.2.)

"In the rather small market we are in there are no true talent agencies," he continued. "We typically use non-talent talent."

After graduating from Louisiana State University with a business major, Julian worked in television promotions and radio sales for eight years before opening Advertir. His two staff members are Gladys Rodriguez—sales assistant/traffic coordinator—and Vanessa Robledo—administrative assistant/office manager (www.Advertir.net).

Is the Texas market more youth-oriented than the United States as a whole? "Somewhat," concluded Julian, "in that Hispanics tend to be younger."

functions as a "distorted mirror"—"a selective reinforcement of only some behaviors and values" to "serve seller's interests" by highlighting "those values that are most readily linked to the available products, that are easily dramatized in advertisements, and that are most reliably responded to by consumers who see the advertisements" (p. 360).

Other scholars have studied this "distorted mirror" concept in non-U.S. cultures. In Chinese TV commercials, Cheng (1997) found modernity, technology, quality and youth were highlighted in 1990 TV commercials, whereas by 1995, "tradition" had replaced "quality" as the dominant value in TV commercials. In Irish TV commercials 1960s–1980s, O'Driscoll (2021) found enjoyment/ leisure, success/status and modernity/technology were highlighted. However, only a few studies on seniors' advertising portrayals deal with TV commercials (Roy & Harwood, 1997).

Seniors in *Time* Magazine Advertisements

An impressive amount of prior advertising research has addressed images in *Time*, providing context for the very recent research in this chapter. Ji and Cooper (2022) provide the model for this chapter, including their choice of *Time* magazine as representing mainstream mass media. The magazine's long history, national circulation and large audience make it a popular medium to represent a national audience. As the magazine nears its 100th birthday (in 2023), this status will evolve and inevitably change.

TIME MAGAZINE

Magazines have served as a national vehicle for selling goods to the U.S. middle class since the 1890s (Shoemaker & Reese, 1996). In 1923, Yale classmates Henry Luce and Briton Hadden founded, in New York City, a new type of magazine, a weekly compendium of national and international news for busy Americans.

From the 1930s to early 1960s, *Time* held its status as the most prominent magazine in America (Baughman, 1998). Thereafter, with competition from network TV news and due to social changes, *Time* declined somewhat in influence. The global recession of 2007–2009 seriously hurt all magazines, including *Time* (Gaille, 2016).

As a money-saving measure, the magazine began publishing more double issues. In 2016, *Time* moved from midtown to downtown Manhattan. Still, as of 2015, print edition revenues were four times higher than the digital-edition revenues (P. Elliott, personal communication, November 17, 2015).

With declines in print circulation, *Time* has gone digital (KAF, 2020). In January 2018, the Meredith Corporation acquired *Time*. As the industry got more unsettled (Felsenthal, 2018), Meredith sold the magazine to Salesforce, an enterprise software company founded by Marc Benioff. Since November 2018, it has been published by Benioff as TIME USA, LLC.

The magazine's filing of required information with the U.S. Postal Service for the issue date of September 21, 2020, includes these statistics: total paid circulation, 1,010,577; total free or nominal rate, 661,889; total distribution, 1,672,466—a clear decline from 2005's circulation of just under four million subscribers, with 150,000 copies sold on newsstands. However, considering pass-along readership, the magazine's ads still reach millions of people.

Research on Time *Ads Depicting Seniors, pre-2000*

An early content analysis that included *Time* (Gantz, Gartenberg & Rainbow, 1980), found, for 1977, that 111 of 1,294 ads (8.6%) showed elderly people. In terms of models in those *Time* ads, only 170 of 3,906 models (4.4%) were coded as elderly—the largest percentage of the seven general-interest publications they studied. The nearly invisible elderly, they conclude, are not considered major consumers. By 1989, elders' presence had increased to 10.2% (Cooper-Chen, Leung & Cho, 1994). McConatha, Schell and McKenna (1999), who looked at a total of 2,505 people in 765 ads in *Time* and *Newsweek* during one year, found infrequent depictions of older adults.

Research on Time *Ads Depicting Seniors, 2000–2019*

The results of Ji and Cooper (2022), the basis for comparison with this chapter's presentation, can be summarized in terms of their abstract:

"This study of 5,796 models pictured in *Time* magazine's advertising over the past 20 years supported Pollay's view of advertising as a 'distorted mirror' that misportrays Americans aged 60 or older. The 590 elder models (overall, 10.2% of the models in ads) steadily increased in visibility over the past 20 years." Ji and Cooper's (2022) research is described here in detail.

Time *Ads Change over Time*

Figure 4.1 shows a steady increase in elders' presence in *Time,* especially after 2015. The next year, 2016, marks the year that the oldest Baby Boomers likely

Percentage of Elders Portrayed in Time Ads 2000-2019

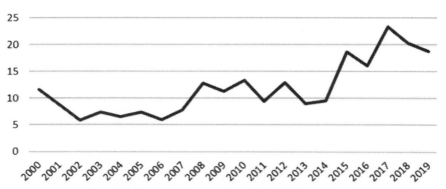

Figure 4.1   From Ji and Cooper (2022). Reprinted by permission of Taylor and Francis Ltd.

felt themselves to have turned somewhat old, at age 70. The highest percentages of elders (more than 15%) appeared in the most recent five years, 2015–2019. The longest run of elders' diminished presence (below 10%) occurred in the early years of the study, 2001–2007. Other factors could be at work, but those initial years are associated with Baby Boomers' pre-elder status, in that they were all still under retirement age (i.e., younger than 65).

Time *Ads vs. the Percentage of Elders in the U.S. Population*

Elders in ads were somewhat underrepresented in relation to their proportion of their population—especially at the beginning (11.6% presence) of the study's 20-year span. Others' research that focused on years before 2000 did not make comparisons with the real world.

Elders Portrayed in Time *Ads Having Visible Infirmities*

Fully 99.5% of models exhibited no infirmity. Ji and Cooper (2022, para. 75) conclude that "ads conveyed no 'admission' on the part of advertisers that older Americans use walkers, canes or wheelchairs or need to convalesce, using an at-home or health-facility hospital bed. Given marketers' persuasive aims—to sell a product or promote a cause—one would not expect altruistic portrayals."

Ji and Cooper (2022) found several limitations to their 20-year study: difficulty in judging models' ages, especially models in their 60s; difficulty of identifying Hispanic models; and inattention to nonphysical infirmities. Alzheimer's

Figure 4.2. The Alzheimer's Association placed this ad in many media outlets, including *Time* magazine, where it appeared on June 13, 2016. Ads showing older African American women have been relatively rare until recently. Used with permission, Alzheimer's Association, 2022.

disease would qualify as an infirmity, but the visual of a doctor, nurse or other care giver with a senior made for clear coding decisions, whereas ads related to Alzheimer's (see Figure 4.2) did not meet the original criteria for coding infirmity.

Seniors' Portrayals in *Time* Ads, 2020 and 2021

METHOD

Exclusive to this chapter are analyses that update the 20-year study outlined in detail above. *Time* published 31 issues in 2020 and 24 issues in 2021. No sampling was done; every ad with people was coded. The Ji and Cooper (2022) method is the same as the original research in this chapter.

Only full-page ads showing photographs of humans (no drawings, paintings or cartoons) were coded. The unit of analysis was a human image with head size at least one quarter-inch high. A maximum of five dominant (by size) human images per ad were included. If an ad pictured, for example, seven young people and two older people, both elders were coded, along with counting the five non-elders. Bodies only partially shown (e.g., just hands or feet) were excluded. For models 60 or older, gender and race (see chapter 9), as well as infirmity and product being advertised, were coded.

ELDER MODEL

The concept of "old age" varies. The United Nations uses age 60 to define a person as older (Office of the United Nations High Commissioner for Refugees, n.d.). Those aged 60 and above can be further divided into "the young old" (people in their 60s and 70s) and "the old old" (85 and above) (Pinsker, 2020). Ji and Cooper (2022) counted models who looked to be 60 or older as elders, based on gray hair, lined or wrinkled skin or whose age was known or implied in the text (Baiocchi-Wagner, 2012; Esswein & Block, 2014; Ylanne, Williams & Wadleigh, 2009).

ADVERTISED PRODUCT

Products had 13 options: clothing/fashion/accessories, health products/health care, automobile, electronics/technology, travel, food/non-alcoholic drink, tobacco, alcohol, financial services, pet-related, home appliance and furniture, entertainment/media and other (Raman et al., 2008; Xue & Ellzey, 2009).

INFIRMITY

An adverse physical condition included coding options of sitting in a wheelchair, being in a hospital bed, exhibiting another infirmity and infirmity not visible.

INTER-CODER RELIABILITY

For the 20-year study, 24 issues (10% of the total 240 issues) were randomly selected for reliability testing between Ji and Cooper. Agreement on who was 60 or over was 81.3%. For the 61 elder images that the two authors identified, agreement was high: gender, 100%; race, 96.7%; product, 86.9%; and infirmity, 100%.

The first author of this book, as a coauthor of the 20-year study, was well versed in coding, as witness the high inter-coder agreements noted above. The 2020–2021 update followed the same methodology as the 20-year analysis, but with some additional insights. Table 4.1 illustrates one of those additional analyses, answering this question:

Q1. How many and what percent of total ads in Time *included at least one senior model?*

Table 4.1 shows that relatively few ads contained images of elders: 19.6% in 2020 and 18.2% in 2021. However, near invisibility had prevailed in earlier years; Gantz, Gartenberg and Rainbow (1980) found, for 1977, that only 8.6% of *Time* ads showed elderly people. By 2005, Lei, Cooper-Chen and Cheng (2007) found an increase, with 17.0% of *Time* ads including elders. Keep in mind the difference between the percent of one or more elders in *ads* versus the percent of elderly *people* in the "ad world."

Table 4.1. Number of *Time* Ads with Seniors vs. Total Number of Ads with People

	2020		2021	
	Frequency	*%*	*Frequency*	*%*
# ads with seniors	46	19.6	38	18.2
# ads with people	235	100	209	100

Table 4.2.   Number of Seniors in *Time* Ads vs. Number of People in *Time* Ads

	2020		2021	
	Frequency	*%*	*Frequency*	*%*
# ads with seniors	53	10.7	50	10.7
# ads with people	496	100	466	100

Q2. How many and what percent of total people in Time *were elderly?*

Table 4.2 shows that, in both 2020 and 2021, 10.7% of human images in ads were elderly. The overall average for the 20-year study found that seniors constituted 10.2% of total models, closely matching the recent update. Over the 20 years, percentages fluctuated of course, with higher percentages in later years. We should keep in mind that the actual presence of elders 60 and over in the U.S. population was 22.6% in 2019, according to the U.S. Census Bureau, but the common criterion of 65 and over results in a smaller percentage (see chapter 1). So "ad world" seniors in 2020 and 2021 receive about half the attention that their presence in the real world would indicate they "should" have. As Paul Irving, chairman of the Milken Institute for the Future of Aging, states, "It's high time to call out ageism in advertising" (Dychtwald, 2021, p. 6).

Q3. How many and what percent of elders in Time *showed visible infirmities?*

Table 4.3 shows that only one model (1.8% of senior models) in 2020 had a visible infirmity—a person using oxygen with a nose cannula. In 2021, an ad for pain medicine appeared twice; it showed an unwell person sitting on a bed wearing bedclothes and slippers. The two ads constituted 4.0% of senior models. Overall, the 20-year study (Ji & Cooper, 2022) found only three elder models (.05%) with visible infirmities. Products that address infirmities were more likely to be advertised in 2020 and 2021 than in prior years.

Table 4.3.   Number/Percent of Seniors in *Time* Ads Depicted with Infirmities

	2020		2021	
	Frequency	*%*	*Frequency*	*%*
# with infirm seniors	1	1.8	2	4.0
total # with seniors	53	100	50	100

Q4. *What advertised products are associated with elder models in* Time?

Table 4.4 shows an overwhelming presence (50.2%) of senior models associated with health products/health care. Those most recent issues of the magazine contrast with the overall percentage (35.0%) of health-related ads in the 20-year study. Still, even that lower percentage ranks as the top product by far 2000–2019. Perhaps the clearest finding of the two studies, taken together, proves the long-term association of old people with drugs, ailments and ill health (Balazs, 1995). An advertising executive commented to this book's authors on that association (see Box 4.1).

The other products with more than a 1% presence show similarities between the two studies: financial services, electronics/technology, travel, entertainment/media, home appliances/furniture (including safe bathtubs). Table 4.4 breaks down Other into two categories, given the phenomenon in 2020–2021 of Asian governments and corporations buying space for ads that look like feature stories ("advertorials"). That category accounts for 13.6% of ads.

A study (Roy & Harwood, 1997) of 778 TV commercials found products associated with the most elders were food/restaurants, retail chains and health/beauty products. Examining various health-related messages in British magazine ads, Ylanne, Williams and Wadleigh (2009) found that aids such as special beds and walk-in baths were the dominant products targeting the elderly.

As the next chapter will show, health/medical advertising has a long history in mainstream media—and an association with elders. The Food and Drug Administration curbed excesses during the years of the *Time* studies described in this chapter, but even today it needs to rein in rogue ads that try to prey on senior citizens.

Table 4.4. Products Associated with Seniors in *Time* Ads

	2020	2021		TOTAL
	# Models	# Models	Total #	%
Health	33	19	52	50.5
Financial services	7	2	9	8.7
Electronics/technology	2	5	7	6.7
Travel	2	3	5	4.8
Entertainment/media	3	0	3	2.9
Home Appliance/furniture	0	3	3	2.9
Other: advertorials	3	11	14	13.6
Other	3	7	10	9.7
Total senior models	53	50	103	100

Box 4.2. Senior Models—
Divisions and Agencies

Bella Agency/40+ Lifestyle Division
270 Lafayette St., Suite 802, New York, NY 10012; 212-965-9200
6430 Sunset Blvd., Suite 460, Los Angeles, CA 90028; 323-462-9191
In 2005, the agency started its 40+ Women Division. In 2011, the New York–based agency opened its Los Angeles office.

IMG Models
304 Park Ave. S, New York, NY 10010; 212-253-8884
With offices in five other major world cities, IMG made news when, in 2019, it hired Iris Apfel, 97, possibly the oldest person signed by a major modeling agency. It represents Maye Musk, born in 1948 (the mother of Elon Musk), who has been modeling for 50 years.

Wilhelmina Models—Sophisticated Women's Division
300 Park Ave S, New York, NY, 10010; 212-473-0700
Established in 1967, the agency represents Nicky Griffin, the oldest model to appear in *Sports Illustrated*'s swimsuit edition. At age 56, the mother of two wore a gold bikini for her cover shot.

Silver Agency (Senior Models Only)
6 Rue SaintClaude, 75003, Paris, France; 33-1-40-20-43-65
Established in 2012 to "represent women and men whose beauty defies time," all its models are over 40. Maybelline featured the agency's Bethany Nagy in a lipstick ad.

Chapter 4. Projects and Exercises

1. Look up the Wendy's "Where's the beef?" Clara Peller ad on YouTube. Do you think it represents a caricature insulting to older women or a proud representation of feistiness? Ask the opinion of people who remember the ad from 1984.
2. Locate copies of *Time* magazine that predate the years of the Ji and Cooper (2022) study, that is, before 2000. Replicate the study for various years; then compare the results with the 2000–2019 results.
3. Locate another general-interest magazine for the years 2020 and 2021. Replicate the method outlined in this chapter and compare the results.
4. Find various ads showing older adults. Show them to 10 people over age 65 and 10 people in their 20s. Note their reactions and compare the two groups' sentiments.
5. Through a library or a subscription, look at current issues of online *Time*. What advertising appears online? Do seniors appear in any of the ads?

#### CHAPTER 5

Medical Advertising's Elder Appeals, Then and Now

"In the kind of work I do, you are surrounded by people who are all younger than you," states 65-year-old Douglas in a TV ad. "I had to get help to stay competitive." Douglas was scared, but when he started taking an over-the-counter pill called Prevagen, "My memory definitely improved. It was a game changer for me." A voiceover then intones, "Prevagen. Healthier brain. Better life." Prevagen ads air regularly on network TV shows with an older audience, such as network evening news programs. They don't invoke scientific proof; they just present personal testimonials.

The testimonial ad replaces an earlier version featuring a bar graph "proving" a rise from 5% to 10% score on recall tasks to 20% on recall tasks after subjects took "an ingredient originally found in jellyfish." In 2012, the original ad prompted the U.S. Food and Drug Administration (FDA) to charge the maker of Prevagen (Quincy Bioscience of Madison, WI) not only with false advertising, but failure to report more than 1,000 serious events, including seizures and strokes. The warning letter disallowed Prevagen's status as a dietary supplement, ruling it a drug; castigated Quincy for violating the federal requirement to get approval when a drug undergoes a clinical trial; and stated that the main ingredient does not come from jellyfish.

According to Robert Shmerling, MD (2021), senior faculty editor of Harvard Health Publishing, "Never mind that the main ingredient in jellyfish (apoaequorin) has no known role in human memory, or that many experts believe supplements like this would most likely be digested in the stomach and never wind up anywhere near the brain. And if apoaequorin is so great, why aren't jellyfish smarter?" At this writing, Prevagen displays in drug stores still tout the presence of apoaequorin as an ingredient, while the bottles claim it "improves memory" (see Figure 5.1).

Figure 5.1. **This pharmacy display shows that Prevagen still advertises apoaequorin, an ingredient in jellyfish that has no known benefits for memory enhancement.**

The FDA closed its case in 2018, saying Quincy had addressed its concerns. The older adults in the new ads, who were paid for their testimonials, are called "content contributors"; these lines of small type run under the ad for about 3 seconds: "These statements have not been evaluated by the FDA. This product is not intended to diagnose, treat, cure or prevent any disease." Prevagen costs $25 for a month's supply, while the "professional formula" costs $90 per month.

The Federal Trade Commission (FTC), however, subsequently sued Quincy, whose sales probably totaled $165 million, 2007–2015, but have likely increased since then (Hamilton, 2021). The case is ongoing at this writing. The FTC regulates over-the-counter drug advertising, and the FTC Act prohibits deceptive ads. The FDA runs a Bad Ad Program for health care providers. The legislation that brings in the FDA— the Federal Food, Drug and Cosmetic Act—occurs when an ad for a prescription drug overstates a drug's benefits or misleads consumers; President Roosevelt signed it in 1938.

The federal Bureau of Chemistry's chief, Harvey Wiley, successfully pushed for the Federal Pure Food and Drugs Act of 1906, known as the Wiley Act. The bureau thereafter prohibited the adulteration of products with harmful ingredients, and labels had to list alcohol, heroin, cocaine and other dangerous ingredients. Before 1906, "Many patent medicines ended up relying on large quantities of morphine or cocaine to give users a high instead of actually healing them" (Panko, 2017).

The Checkered History of Drug Ads

This chapter aims to impart understanding of the state of remedy ads aimed at the elderly before the FDA protected them. Steven Johnson (2021b), in his TED talk "How Humanity Doubled Life Expectancy in a Century," credits as a "prime mover [in extending life] large bureaucratic institutions"—specifically the FDA. "A lot of medical historians believe that all-in-all pharmaceutical drugs were a net negative" until the 1940s, Johnson says.

As Young (1961, p. 247) states, "Prior to 1906, the only inhibition upon American patent medicine proprietors, except for an occasional critical article, was self-restraint. This did not prove an adequate force for the protection of the medicine-consuming public." What kinds of claims appeared in the mass media before 1906 (i.e., in newspapers)? What kind of appeals did advertisers use? The contemporary Prevagen ad cited above uses a fear appeal. Can we see parallels between an ad like today's Prevagen and pre-1906 ads? What has changed? What remains the same?

Aging and Disease in 1860

According to Berry and Barnett (2019), "In 1850, medical diagnostics were rudimentary, autopsies were rare and reliable data scarce. The nosology [classification of human diseases] created for the 1850 Mortality Census, then, was inevitably crude."

In 1850, the average life expectancy of 38.3 years reflected the death of about half of children by age 5 and maternal mortality in childbirth; however, if a woman survived to age 60, she lived on average to age 74 in the 1850–1930 period. Many men even attained longevity similar to that of the present day: John Adams lived to age 90; Ben Franklin, to 84; Thomas Jefferson and Paul

Revere, to 83; and George Wythe, to 80. George Washington likely would have lived beyond age 67, except for blood loss due to treatments that doctors used on him.

The prevalent practice of bloodletting, with its history dating back to ancient Egypt, "followed from humoral doctrines, especially Galen's theory of 'plethora'—the idea that fevers, apoplexy and headache resulted from excessive buildup of blood" (Porter, 2003, p. 115). Use of blood-sucking leeches for maladies including hemorrhoids continued up through the 1800s. In the mid-1800s, "the familiar premise [was] that all disease had but one cause"—bad blood (Young, 1961, p. 79).

Porter (2003), a medical historian, provides further insights into practices and beliefs of the time frame of this chapter, the mid-1800s: "Strong sedatives, analgesics and narcotics [were] newly marketed by the nineteenth-century pharmaceutical companies" (p. 39); rather than "cynical swindlers, many were fanatics about their techniques or nostrums" (p. 45). Most, however, simply wanted to sell their wares. In the 1800s, "drugs became production-line items" (p. 102) that increased sales through publicity.

Advertising for patent medicines and other products "supplied more than half of the revenue that a 19th-century newspaper needed" (Donald Shaw, personal communication, June 21, 2021). "Ads have always been a key part of newspapers' pages. News researchers have had to train themselves not to look at the ads, as they are so interesting. Reading them is like walking back into the world at that time."

Studies of Early Drug Advertising

Stallings (1992) states that U.S. advertising began to achieve momentum in the 1700s. By the 1800s, prosperity had increased people's ability to buy drugs touted by "bold and exaggerated" advertising (p. 211). Distribution means also improved. At the same time, "Budding advertising agencies transferred copy from entrepreneurs to newspapers and magazines" (p. 212).

Stallings takes a cultural/analytical approach, stating that marketing of drugs and medicines, which originated from "an English legacy" (p. 218), has "changed over time with American cultural transformation" (p. 217). The U.S. 17th-century English legacy included "embellished and overstated broadsides" (p. 218). Throughout its early history, advertising "reminded generations of the precariousness of health . . . through exaggeration (rarely understated)" (p. 218).

Young's (1961) comprehensive book *Toadstool Millionaires* chronicles the history of patent medicines before federal regulation curbed their advertising excesses. He ascribes importance to such study as affording "insight into an anti-rational approach to one of the key problems of life" and presents as an object lesson the legions of Americans who fell for pre-regulation quackery throughout "the age of the common man" (p vii). According to Young (p. 70), Americans were "ignorant victims of their own credulity," susceptible to testimonials, "whether or not [the recommender] was qualified to speak."

Attacks on the press for running egregious ads for unproven or harmful remedies, "the scandalous nature of some of the copy it accepted for pay," prompted publishers to blame the customer; newspapers accepted ads whereby "any competitor was free to advertise, pointing out the weakness of rival remedies" (Young 1961, p. 82). Small papers justified such ads by pointing out that they enabled the paper to sell for less due to ad revenues. Indeed, some papers' "schizoid policy" resulted in editorial content criticizing the very ads in the same issue (p. 83). "In the eyes of physicians, the guilt of the newspaper editor was second only to that of the nostrum maker" (p. 84).

The producers of the quack remedies "hired hack writers" to create the overblown ad copy (p. 87). An outraged congressman noted that one successful toadstool millionaire had spent $100,000 on advertising in one year (p. 88) at a time when a quart of milk cost 4 cents.

PERSUASIVE APPEALS

Young (1961) presents a qualitative analysis based on his familiarity with years of pre-1906 remedy advertising. Overarching was the idea that "there were soon more pills and potions than Americans could swallow conveniently. The medicine man's key task became . . . persuading ailing citizens to buy his particular brand" (p. 166). He outlines components for quacks' marketing success:

- *Product identity* via relentless repetition, even placing multiple ads in one issue of a newspaper.
- *Uniqueness* via a memorable name with distinctive type and graphics.
- *Credibility* via medical credentials, whether real or fabricated, and user testimonials, whether from respected persons like clergy or "humble citizens . . . [who often] did not exist, except in the imagination of the copywriter" or whose praise could be "purchased for a pittance" (p. 188).
- *Denigration* of practicing doctors: "Their treatment was costly, his was cheap . . . [and] quick. Their approaches were cumbersome, his were simple" (p. 169).
- *Simplistic* promotion of ailments with a one-shot remedy, whether vegetable or mineral.

- *Exoticism* via emphasis on the faraway, whether in time (e.g., ancient Egypt) or geography (e.g., Turkey, Japan and China, or populations distant from major U.S. cities, e.g., Native Americans). Marcellus (2008) agrees that Native Americans' nature-based knowledge of cures constituted one theme of drug advertising in the 1800s: the noble savage.
- *Instilling of fear* via exaggeration of small symptoms, turning "normal physiological phenomena into dread signs of incipient pain and death" (p. 184).
- *Flaunting of statistics*, e.g., "efficacy for ten years" (p. 186), success in numerous locales or "cures so numerous" (p. 187).

In sum, "the patent medicine industry ran the gamut of appeals to human psychology. Critics might rant, the judicious might grieve, but the nostrum promoter pursued his wily way" (p. 189).

THE NEED FOR REFORM

Young (1961) emphasizes "the significance of federal regulation" (p. 247). Consider the situation before 1906, including in 1860, our focus year:

> Before 1906, the most respectable proprietors considered it not improper to market medicines containing unmentioned narcotics— like Mrs. Winslow's Soothing Syrup—or a high proportion of alcohol—like Hostetter's Bitters. Nor did they feel any great compulsion to restrain creative claims. . . . At least kidney disease or cancer would not find its way into the advertising of large-scale manufacturers today. (pp. 247–248)

Further, states Young (1961),

> Medical matters fuzzy [in the 1800s] have been clarified by modern research. Many quack claims that then could not be combatted with scientific certainty can now be shown to be ridiculous. Pseudomedical promotion of remedies for diabetes or syphilis, for example, cannot today possess the specious plausibility that their predecessor once enjoyed. Modern medical science, of course, is an indispensable bulwark to effective governmental regulation. (p. 251)

Petty (2019) profiles one particular vegetable-based 19th-century medicine, a pain killer, as a precursor to modern branding techniques. Sales of millions of bottles of the most popular medicines ended when regulations limited advertisers' ability to tout cure-all claims in the early 1900s. Porter (2003) agrees that, without regulation, most drug manufacturers took advantage of public gullibility:

> With the rise of the consuming public, demand welled up for many sorts of healing and commercial society provided openings which nostrum-mongers, rejuvenators and cancer-curers rushed to fill. The craving for sure-fire cures produced 'toadstool millionaires' galore, eager to bestow magnetic, electrical, chemical or herbal cures on the desperate or credulous. Proprietary medicines won loyal followings. (p. 46)

Concludes Young (1961), "As he did in the 19th century, so does man yearn desperately for things that cannot be" (p. 253)— simple, sure-fire cures. An 1800s experienced ad man advised: "You must write your advertisements to catch damned fools" (p. 255). The following questions build on but delve more specifically into pre-regulated remedy ads than the writers above by focusing on the elderly.

Method: Studying 1860 Remedy Ads

This book's first author chose to study the year 1860, which represented a maturing nation of 33 U.S. states. As home to more than 31 million people, the United States had experienced, according to that year's census, a major population increase of 35.6% since the census of 10 years earlier. The nearly 4 million enslaved persons counted as three-fifths of a person for taxation and U.S. House apportionment. As historian Kinsley (1943, p. 105) states, "The year 1860 was one of the most important in American history, for it saw the nomination and election of Lincoln and the onset of the Civil War." The war actually began on April 12, 1861.

By 1860, telegraph communication was well developed. The postal service, which had issued its first stamps in 1847, began the Pony Express in 1860. (The Sacramento paper in this study advertised quick-service delivery of a letter to New York—in only eight days). The Industrial Revolution reached its full flowering by 1860, whereby unskilled labor could assemble items with interchangeable parts, such as sewing machines and typewriters. The assembly-line factories attracted workers to cities, where wages higher than on farms and more leisure meant people had time to read newspapers and money to buy advertised goods. Gristmills and sawmills proliferated.

Newspapers, the mass medium of the day, constituted the vehicle by which advertisers reached the public. The four newspapers in this chapter represent a geographic swath across the nation in four diverse states and city sizes:

- In Illinois, the 4th-largest state, Chicago (pop. 112,172, 9th-largest U.S. city)—*Press and Tribune*
- In Virginia, the 5th-largest state, Alexandria (pop. 12,652, 75th-largest U.S. city)—*Alexandria Gazette and Virginia Advertiser*
- In Texas, the 23rd-largest state, San Antonio (pop. 8,235, largest town in Texas)—*Daily Ledger and Texan*
- In California, the 26th-largest state, Sacramento (pop. 13,785, 67th-largest U.S. city)—*Sacramento Daily Union*

Preliminary research showed that all four newspapers published throughout 1860. To generate a sample, one week per month was randomly chosen (from first through fourth); from all the days of the week that a particular paper published, one day was randomly chosen (only the California paper published a Saturday edition; the three others had a Monday-through-Friday schedule). Papers in the 19th century did not publish on Sunday (Donald Shaw, personal communication, June 21, 2021). The selected days included, from east to west location:

Alexandria Gazette and Virginia Advertiser—fourth Wednesday
Press and Tribune (Chicago)—second Monday
Daily Ledger and Texan—third Monday
Sacramento Daily Union—first Saturday

If a target date's issue of these 160-year-old newspapers was not available or illegible, the next day for which an issue existed was analyzed. Unlike for a news content study, substitution for a missing target issue did not create problems of misrepresented data (due to the repetitiveness of ads issue after issue).

All four newspapers contained four pages each day. The Texas and Virginia papers' pages were divided into six columns; the California paper, seven columns; and the Illinois paper, eight columns. All content was confined within a column, making 1860 ads look like today's classifieds; no news articles' headlines were deployed across several columns. Regulations on type size for paid ads meant that designers used "drop capitals, repetition, and acrostics to produce patterns" (McFall, 2015, p. 13).

For the *Alexandria Gazette*, the ads under the large-type heading (usually on page 1) DRUGS, CHEMICALS & C were noted, even though many of the products were "C" (cetera, Latin for "other"), rather than drugs. For the other three newspapers, the author visually searched through all advertising for drugs, medicines and remedies. No doctor's office ads were included. Included ads had to address elder-specific conditions or ailments that affected the old as well as the young (no baby medicines or those for younger, i.e., nursing, women were included).

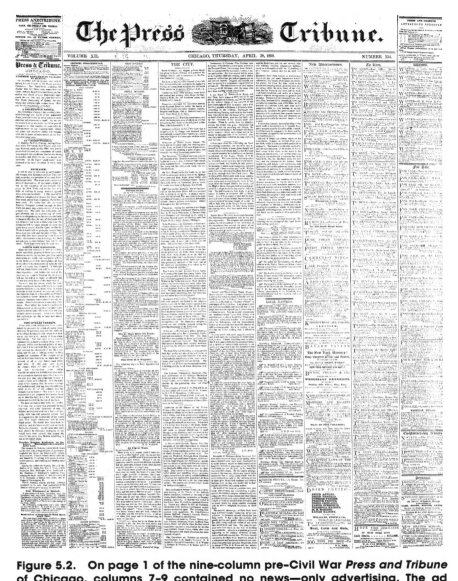

Figure 5.2. On page 1 of the nine-column pre-Civil War *Press and Tribune* of Chicago, columns 7-9 contained no news—only advertising. The ad section, which also took up the lower part of column 6, included an ad for Dr. Sanford's Liver Invigorator—one of the most advertised remedies in the years before the FDA controlled outrageous claims (just above the ad that reads, "Stoves, Stoves").

The *Chicago Press and Tribune* (see Figure 5.2) stands out as the most prominent newspaper of the four, encompassing the journalism icon Joseph Medill, as well as a member of the Scripps family, editor John Locke Scripps, in the period of this chapter. It soon ranked "next to the *New York Tribune* in influence" (Kinsley, 1943, p. 33); by 1857, daily circulation had increased to 4,000. Alexandria, Virginia, holds a prominent place in pharmaceutical advertising history as home to the Stabler-Leadbeater Apothecary Museum, a drug sales and manufacturing business opened in 1775.

Appeals used by newspaper ads, adapted from Young (1961), are defined as follows:

- *Repetition*: relentless replication of advertising for the product in various venues over time
- *Fear*: description of a dreaded outcome that might occur without the remedy
- *Exoticism*: references to Indians or persons/ingredients from Asia or the Middle East
- *Credibility*: use of credentials, especially "doctor," or testimonials from users, often respected
- *Statistics*: use of numbers (cures, years) or citing a range of locales where the product is used
- *Hyperbole*: exaggerated, overblown language touting the remedy's powers
- *Uniqueness*: use of unusual graphic devices to attract readers' attention
- *Multiplicity*: citing of many maladies the remedy can cure, simplifying the buyer's choices
- *Descriptive*: no particular appeal beyond a statement of use and where to obtain the product

Elder-specific conditions included gray hair, baldness, hearing loss, osteoporosis and rheumatism.

RESULTS: 1860 REMEDY ADS

1a. What remedy advertisements are aimed specifically at elders?

Table 5.1 shows that hair-related products by far dominate elder-targeted ads. Each of the four newspapers carried at least one brand of what in 1860 was called a "hair restorative." The Texas newspaper also carried ads for Argyl Bitters, with the following wording aimed at elders:

> Persons advanced in life, and feeling the hand of Time weighing
> heavily upon them, with all its attendant ills, will find in the use of

Table 5.1. Type of Advertised Product, 1860 Newspapers: Elder-Specific Ailments

Venue	# Insertions	Product	Ailment	Appeal
VA	1	Wood's Hair Restorative*	Not stated	Descriptive
	2	Eau Athenienne Hair Restorer	Baldness, graying	Hyperbole
IL	1	Prof. Wood's Hair Restorative*	Baldness, graying	Hyperbole, credibility
TX	10	Argyl Bitters	Aging	Hyperbole, statistics
	6	Wood's Hair Restorative*	Baldness, graying	Hyperbole, credibility
CA	4	Fish's Hair Restorative	Baldness, graying	Hyperbole
	1	Cristadoro's Hair Dye	Graying	Hyperbole, credibility
TOTAL	25			

*The product was variously called Wood's or Prof. Wood's; ads differed in specificity.

the Bitters an elixir, that will instill new life into the veins, restore in a measure, the energy and ardor of more youthful days, build up their shrunken forms and give health and happiness in their remaining years.

It is a well-established fact that fully one-half of the female portion of our population are seldom in the enjoyment of good heath. . . . Bitters are especially recommended.

1b. What ailments affecting elders do the products purport to cure?

Argyl Bitters, advertised heavily in the Texas newspaper, claimed nothing less than being a fountain of youth. The hair restoratives in all newspapers promised to cure both grayness and baldness. The California paper carried an ad reading: "Fish's Infallible Hair Restorative Will restore gray hair to its original color, whether Black, Brown or Auburn. It prevents the hair from falling off and cures baldness."

The same paper carried an ad for Cristadoro's hair dye, promising that those whose hair is "grizzled by sickness or time" will "be made beautiful" after using the product, which is "certified pure and harmless by Dr. Chilton, the most distinguished chemist in the United States."

1c. What appeals do the advertisers use in ads targeting elders?

All ads for hair restoratives used *hyperbole* (the Virginia paper's ad for Wood's Hair Restorative, however, stated only its name). The word *infallible* in the Fish's ad quoted above exemplifies hyperbole, as does the phrase "most distinguished chemist in the United States." Argyl Bitters promised, in flights of hyperbole, "to build up [elders'] shrunken forms" and engender happiness; the ad's reference to "one-half" of all women exemplifies the use of *statistics* (without any proof). The terms *professor* and *doctor* attempt to impart *credibility* to the hair products. All the hair products that purport to alleviate both baldness and graying exemplify a *multiplicity* appeal.

2. Do more advertisements target all adults than target elders specifically?

Yes. Table 5.2 shows that the newspapers carried 241 insertions for products targeted at all adults, compared to only 25 insertions for products aimed at elders (see Table 5.1). Interestingly, the newspaper in the smallest city (San Antonio) carried the most ads, perhaps because of a lack of local pharmacies that mixed up concoctions (like Leadbetter's and Stabler's in Alexandria) or a lack of doctors, creating the need for self-medication.

3. Does the repetition of brand-name products occur across the United States?

Table 5.3 shows that six products repeated their ads across the nation. (Of course many ads repeated regularly within individual newspapers, due to contracts for specific-length runs.) We should note that Hostetter's Bitters, a national brand advertised in three of the four newspapers in this study, contained a large proportion of alcohol (Young, 1961, p. 247). The product that used the most sweeping approach advertised in all four newspapers, Sanford's Liver Invigorator;

Table 5.2.   Number of Advertised Products, 1860 Newspapers: General Adult Ailments

Venue	# Insertions	Notes
VA	54	Alexandria had many druggists, whose ads were often lists of their wares
IL	17	The largest of the four cities, Chicago had few newspaper medicine ads
TX	108	San Antonio was the smallest, most isolated city of the four
CA	62	Sacramento was and is the capital of California; statehood was ratified 1850
TOTAL	241	

Table 5.3. Adult-Targeted Remedy Advertising, 1860 Newspapers: U.S.-Wide Repetition

Venues Carrying Ad	Product
TX, VA, IL, CA	Sanford's (Liver) Invigorator
TX, IL, CA	Sanford's Family Cathartic Pills
TX, VA, IL	Brown's Bronchial Troches
TX, VA, IL,	(Prof.) Wood's Hair Restorative
VA, IL, CA	Hostetter's (Stomach) Bitters
VA, IL	Moffat's Vegetable Life Pills and Phoenix Bitters

Sanford's Family Cathartic Pills often appeared below it. The Invigorator not only advertised itself nationally, but it bombarded the reader with no less than five appeals (discussed in detail in the conclusions).

4. What appeals do advertisements targeting adults use as persuasion to induce sales?

Table 5.4 shows exaggeration (*hyperbole*) as the primary trait of remedy ads, which touted their products' efficacy with superlatives that seem almost comical today. In the California newspaper, Rowler's Infallible Rheumatism Medicine (which also cured syphilis, ulcers, swollen glands and other ills) was called "unequal in the known world," while Dr. Hall's Balsam "is the strongest certified medicine in the world" for curing tuberculosis and various ailments, "giving immediate relief and imparting a cheerful sensation of returning health and strength"—without any opium. In the Virginia newspaper, an ad for Moffat's Vegetable Life Pills and Phoenix Bitters touted "the high and envied celebrity

Table 5.4. Adult-Targeted Remedy Advertising, 1860 Newspapers: Appeals

Appeal	# of Usages by State				
	VA	IL	TX	CA	TOTAL
Hyperbole	18	7	78	43	146
Multiple usages*	25	9	39	42	115
Credibility**	10	10	50	40	110
Statistics***	4	3	20	12	39
Graphic devices	0	6	18	13	37
Exoticism	1	0	0	4	5
Fear	0	0	0	0	0

*Indicates claims of curing two or more conditions, offering simplicity (no need for other drugs).
**Includes both the use of titles like "doctor" or "professor" and published testimonials.
***Includes time in years as well as geographic ranges (e.g., across the South and West).
Note: Ads without any type of appeal (i.e., merely mentioning the remedy's name) were omitted unless the name itself indicated the purported cure (e.g., Wood's Hair Restorative).

which these prominent Medicines have acquired for their invaluable efficacy," while an ad for Hunnewell's Universal Cough Remedy (which contained "not a particle of opium") promised to "leave the patient in a perfect natural state." The Chicago newspaper ran an ad for Atwood's Quinine Tonic Bitters, calling it modestly "the best tonic ever offered to the public."

Regarding *multiplicity* of usages, the second most prevalent advertising appeal, Moffat's Vegetable Life Pills and Phoenix Bitters, stands as an extreme example; it could cure asthma, rheumatism, bladder and kidney problems, fever, liver complaints, colic, piles, colds, coughs, "corrupt humors," dropsy (edema), dyspepsia, skin eruptions, flatulence, fever, ague, gout, giddiness, headaches, impure blood, jaundice, loss of appetite, "mercurial diseases," night sweats, "nervous debility," pains in the limbs, "rush of blood to the head," scrofula (a type of tuberculosis) and worms. The ad ran in the Virginia newspaper.

Credibility, the third in usage by advertisers, took the form of real or self-bestowed credentials in such products as Prof. Wood's Hair Restorative, Dr. Browning's Fever & Ague Mixture, Dr. Hall's Balsam, Dr. Montardo's Miraculous Pain Killer and Dr. Pereira's Great Italian Remedy. Another form involved testimonials, including those from respected persons, such as an ad for Brown's Bronchial Troches in the Texas newspaper that printed testimonials from six men: clergymen in New York, Ohio, Tennessee and Missouri; a doctor in Boston; and a professor in Georgia.

Another form entailed early attempts at brand identity/integrity. An ad in the California newspaper for Rosenbaum's Celebrated Stomach Bitters cautioned buyers "not to be deceived by a cheap and worthless article . . . called Rosencliff's Bitters [which is] calculated to deceive the unwary." Hostetter's Bitters, also advertised in the California paper, stated that a "good article will always triumph over any pretended imitators." A separate Hostetters's ad in a different issue of the same newspaper warned of "harpies who subsist by pirating" and selling imitations "at a low price."

Fourth in prevalence, *statistics* could cite years of customer sales, such as 50 years for Dr. Pereira's Great Italian Remedy (for "private diseases"), advertised in the California newspaper; by contrast, the more modest Diarrhoea Cordial, advertised in the Virginia newspaper, "has been in use for 8 years." Geographic reach over many areas characterized ads such as another ad for Hostetter's Bitters, sold "from Maine to Texas, from the shores of the Atlantic to the Pacific," in the California newspaper.

One of the *graphic* devices that advertisers used to catch attention in the confines of narrow columns was a vertical bar with the product name "Sanford's" running perpendicular to the ad copy. Other devices included a stair-step listing of ailments or small artwork logos (such as a lozenge shape). The Illinois newspaper carried an ad with the brand name Cephall's Pills arched upward within the column, while underneath the brand, the words "All kinds of head-aches" arched downward within the column, looking like a hammock.

Finally, only four examples of *exoticism* were found. In the Virginia news-paper, an ad for Inpectine, the Persian Fever Charm, related the story of a miraculous combination of medicinal herbs brought back by "a friend who has been a great traveler in Persia and the Holy Land"; the herbs, used "in Persia for thousands of years," cured the traveler of "a severe attack of Fever and Ague." In the California newspaper, three ads used the Noble Savage approach (Young, 1961, p. 177) with a product called Old Sachem Bitters and Wigwam Tonic.

Only one appeal was absent from the 25 elder-specific product insertions plus the 241 adult-ailment product insertions. *Fear* did not characterize any of the 1860 ads.

DISCUSSION AND CONCLUSIONS: THEN

This study of 266 19th-century patent-medicine advertisements addresses the psychological truism that, in the absence of FDA and FTC protections, the most relied-upon psychology was an assumption of gullibility and public trust in exaggerated claims (*hyperbole*). However, that appeal did not preclude others from being used in ads.

A quintessential example of an 1860, pre-FDA ad is Sanford's Liver Invigo-rator, which advertised across the United States, from Virginia to California—the only product in this study to advertise in all four newspapers. Moreover, Sanford's used the most appeals, five, of any product in the study. If successful in stopping the reader with graphics, the copywriter then used four other appeals to induce purchase (example from the *Daily Ledger and Texan*, San Antonio, Monday, March 19, 1860, p. 3):

- Hyperbole: the Invigorator "never debilitates; [it cures those] who had given up all hope of relief"
- Credibility: *respected title*—S. T. Sanford, M.D.—and *testimonials*—"all who use it are giving their testimony in its favor"
- Multiple usages: [the Invigorator cures] cholera, sour stomach, female weakness
- Statistics: the Invigorator "has cured thousands; [it cures migraines] in 20 minutes"

Curing cholera, an acute diarrheal disease caused by a bacterium that infects people who ingest contaminated food or water, requires rehydration therapy and antibiotics. It requires a medical, not a personal, diagnosis. If not properly treated, cholera can kill, as it did in India 1817 to 1860, with more than 15 million victims. Before the FDA, products like Sanford's Invigorator could irresponsibly claim to cure rather than address the cause. Antibiotics did not arrive until 1928 to treat bacterial infections.

Not only the irresponsibility of false claims, but the unrelated nature of the ailments that the medicines purported to cure strikes the 21st-century reader. Even the advertisers themselves pointed out the overblown nature of medical claims. Moffat's Vegetable Life Pills and Phoenix Bitters in the Virginia newspaper referred to "the usual practice of puffing," but exempted the pills themselves as being so reliable as to make puffery "unnecessary." In 1860, "the unscrupulous nostrum promoter could not then be caught and punished for his transgressions" (Young, 1961, p. 249); today, of course, an unproven cure for cancer cannot be advertised.

DISCUSSION AND CONCLUSIONS: NOW

Today, the FDA, FTC and USPS can wage war against such promoters, including their deceptive labeling practices, and win. The history of post-1906 legal cases and regulations lies beyond the scope of this history chapter. However, the Prevagen case outlined at the beginning of this chapter holds some valuable lessons.

Unlike today, 19th-century advertisers did not need to resort to the psychology of fear. Today, that appeal in elder-targeted ads is one replacement for hyperbole. From 1953 to about 1975, "Fear was the primary focus of research" (Witte & Allen, 2000) in advertising. Today's Prevagen ad noted above, whereby an older employee shows fear of competition from younger coworkers, relies on that psychological approach. Indeed, all Prevagen ads play on fear of losses that aging will bring: the ability to remember details, "sharpness," quickness in recall.

Prevagen seems to have adapted the advice of Witte and Allen (2000) for successful public health campaigns. Their findings include: emphasize magnitude of harm (I may lose my job); emphasize similarities with target audience (real elderly give testimonials); make threat likely to happen (if you're old, your memory may start to decline); make the recommended corrective response easy (you just need to buy it at the drugstore).

Other recent examples of elder-specific drug deception stand out. In 2020, sellers of ReJuvenation, who deceptively claimed their pill could cure certain age-related ailments, agreed to provide funds so the FTC could send refunds to consumers who bought the product (Quantum Wellness, 2020). Furthermore, the FTC also ordered refunds in April 2020 from the makers of Neurocet, Regenify and Resetigen-D because of "deceptive marketing, making unsubstantiated claims" that the three could treat "certain age-related health conditions" (Bilodeau, 2022, p. 8).

So the cautions regrading non-presentation drugs aimed at the older U.S. population remain in place. The FDA has noted that older people use more prescription drugs and watch more television than younger people (Scott, 2016). Pharmaceutical manufacturers spend more on marketing than on research and development (Farley, 2020). As Young (1961, p. 165) says, the "psychology of patent medicine advertising is important because of both its priority and its variety."

Chapter 5. Projects and Exercises

1. Duplicate the method in this chapter for pre-1906 medical ads in a newspaper that used to be published in your area.
2. Look up online and analyze all ads in Prevagen's series of testimonials. What kind of persons are speaking about Prevagen? What do they say about effectiveness? (E.g., "It worked for me.")
3. Categorize the ads in recent issues of *AARP The Magazine* or *AARP Bulletin*. How many ads appear? What products are being sold? What percent of models have gray hair?
4. In a major newspaper such as the *New York Times*, find elder-targeted ads for products and services endorsed by celebrities that appeared during the 1970s or 1980s. How would you categorize the celebrity endorsers (sports, film, business or other fields)?
5. Choose one specific ad targeting senior citizens in the 1970s from a magazine such as *People* and reinvent it to fit into a social media platform (use your social media and digital skills).

Part III

PUBLIC RELATIONS AND MARKETING

CHAPTER 6

Creating Effective Senior-Market Messages

"One of the greatest lessons I've learned in marketing to and communicating with seniors is the importance of language and word choice," states Kelsey Knoedler Perri, public relations director at Road Scholar (formerly Elderhostel), a travel nonprofit (see Box 6.1).

> People over 50 don't like to be called "seniors," "senior citizens," "older adults," "elders," "elderly," "aged," etc. If ever I post on Road Scholar's Facebook page using words like *senior* or *older adults*, I always get negative comments. So, for branding purposes, we try to stay away from those terms. We use the term *Boomers and beyond*, but that term won't be accurate forever. You have to be mindful that language evolves and connotations change.
>
> Boomers don't think of themselves as "old" or even, often, as grandparents. Look at the trend of grandparents choosing other nicknames, like "Gigi" or "Glamma." When Boomers think of "seniors" or "retirement," they think of their parents' generation, and they don't feel like they can relate. Seniors today are more adventurous and active: physically, socially, and intellectually. Our participants don't "age gracefully," they "#AgeAdventurously." As a marketer, trends like this can work in your favor. We launched an "Age Adventurously" social media campaign in 2018 that was a huge success.
>
> On the flipside, you also need to make sure that you're clearly communicating what you do and who you are. And, truly, Road Scholar is an organization for seniors. There can be a tradeoff when you opt for branded words on your website in terms of search engine optimization (SEO). When someone is searching online for a travel company for people over 50, they're most likely searching using the term "senior," so if we avoid using that word on our website, we miss out on a lot of organic search traffic. So we try to find a

Box 6.1. What's in a Name?
Elderhostel's Rebranding

Elderhostel was founded in 1975 as a not-for-profit educational organization for older adults by friends Marty Knowlton and David Bianco, who were driven by a mission. That mission and the community that the organization served never changed, but the organization did evolve over the years. When Elderhostel's first programs launched in New Hampshire in 1975, 220 pioneering participants attended lectures on college campuses and stayed in the dorms. By 1980, the organization was hosting more than 20,000 participants on programs in all 50 states and most Canadian provinces, and by 1986, that number grew to 100,000 lifelong learners.

By 2001, Elderhostel was offering learning adventures in more than 100 countries around the world, and participants were more likely to stay in a hotel than a dorm room. "Add to that the emerging Baby Boomer generation attitudes about the term 'elder,'" said Kelsey Knoedler Perri, public relations coordinator. "It began to feel as if 'Elderhostel' no longer accurately represented the organization's identity as the world leader in educational travel." So, to appeal to new audiences and express the real essence of their learning adventures, "Elderhostel" became "Road Scholar" (personal communication, April 4, 2022).

balance—using "senior" in meta descriptions or as a paid ad keyword but avoiding it in heavily branded marketing or communications to audiences who already know us. (personal communication, April 4, 2022)

"We are big on language," agrees Gretchen Likins, who has served for 11 years as the admissions/public relations coordinator at Carol Woods, a 500-person retirement community in Chapel Hill, NC (personal communication, March 23, 2022). "We say 'older adults,' 'higher levels of support' and 'living with dementia'; we don't say 'assisted living' or 'patients.' Language comes before action. We use purposeful words." Given that Carol Woods can accommodate only about 30 new residents each year, Likins concentrates not on marketing but on informative messaging, such as a weekly 30-minute program that airs live on Facebook for the community's 1,500-person wait list.

Most other SilverComm professionals, however, do practice persuasive marketing. These professionals would do well to integrate generational marketing (see chapter 1) into their message strategies.

or a service. Campaigns reach out to target audiences through a combination of media outlets and social media platforms; they aim to positively affect audiences' perception of a product or service, to encourage them to act on the message and usually to make a purchase. Although U.S. senior citizens have spending power, marketers have seen them as merely people "either in the louche [rakish] leisure of a Viagra ad or the frail dependence of a Life Alert spot" (Purtill, 2021, para. 8). Many campaigns targeting senior citizens still focus on their needing physical assistance. In fact, they resent portrayals as "old" and "stupid," particularly during the COVID-19 pandemic (Graham, 2021).

Campaigns should focus on specific demographic segments. Steve Page, president of the agency Giant Partners, explained that senior citizens in their mid-60s and above will willingly buy good products at affordable prices that benefits them in some way. Page (2022) also advised marketing campaigners to create messages employing hype and buzzwords, since senior citizens respond to compelling emotional stories invoking scary scenarios, such as loss of independence and effects on family members.

The previous chapter described the fear appeal that nonprescription Prevagen used in addressing seniors. Indeed, Bartikowski, Laroche and Richard (2019) found, after analyzing 4,155 print ads, that drug/medical products was the category most prone to the use of fear appeals.

MODERNIZED MESSAGES: VIAGRA AND BEYOND

The year 2017 ushered in a marketing shift—away from reliance on consumers' age and gender/toward consumers' attitudes and purchasing behavior (Davis, 2017; Lafayette, 2019). For example, a Mercedes-Benz ad during Super Bowl LI of 2017 (see Figure 6.1) featured 1969's *Easy Rider* star Peter Fonda and Steppenwolf's song "Born to Be Wild"; Fonda, then age 77, ends the commercial driving off in his luxury car, after which the words "Built to be wild" appear (Luttner, 2017). The luxury car brand aimed to connect with, in particular, "older Boomers with money" (Davis, 2017, para. 2).

Throughout 2017, major marketing campaigns featured senior celebrities. Covergirl's campaign with the message of "I Am What I Make Up" featured Elon Musk's mother, Maye (born 1948); Honda's "Power of Dreams" Super Bowl ad featured Robert Redford, 80, and comic book creator Stan Lee, 94, among other A-listers. A strategic shift in customized marketing targeted senior citizens (Lafayette, 2019).

The revolution in customization actually began in 1998. Ads for Pfizer's Viagra, the first drug to treat "erectile dysfunction" (ED), not only began speaking about the heretofore unspeakable condition but also evolved a marketing

Figure 6.1. 2017 Mercedes Campaign for Senior Citizens (Still captures from YouTube: https://www.youtube.com/watch?v=eGYIxORSu1o).

strategy for men in their 60s and above. Viagra, which ushered in a sexual and social revolution, was dubbed "a wonder of the modern age" by *The New York Times* and "the pill that thrills" by the *San Francisco Chronicle* (Irvine, 2006, p. 39). Evolving Viagra messages embedded in its two-decade campaigns demonstrate that brands need to reflect changing social viewpoints, opinions and expectations, including a greater engagement with the target senior audience in discussing private and emotional issues. The Viagra messages have evolved from 1998 to 2018 as follows:

1. Courage: something shared by countless Americans
2. Rebranding of impotence
3. Male enhancement
4. Rebranding of erectile dysfunction (ED)
5. The romance drug
6. Let the dance begin
7. Love life again
8. Step up to the plate
9. The blue pill

Viagra's first 1998 campaign hired former Republican leader of the Senate Bob Dole as a spokesman, conveying the message: "You know, it's a little embarrassing to talk about ED," he said in that early Viagra commercial, "but it's so important to millions of men and their partners that I decided to talk about it publicly" (Garber, 2018). The Viagra marketing messages represented the beginnings of a brand of radical honesty, connecting erectile dysfunction to control and performance, but its messaging strategy has undergone a strategic transformation by repositioning the message from sexual fulfilment to emotional relief (WARC, 2020). A 2020 Viagra marketing campaign, titled "Don't Let Your Life Get in the Way of Your Love Story," emotionally and compassionately tells the story of a couple struggling to maintain their sexual relations as the complications of everyday life threaten to compromise intimacy (see https://www.youtube.com/watch?v=L3BusCaKYcQ).

Post-COVID-19 Messaging

In March 2022—two years after the coronavirus outbreak upended life in the United States—senior citizens confronted rapid digital transformation more than ever as they adapted to constantly changing virtual and online landscapes (Gramlich, 2022). According to a Pew Research survey, adoption of key technologies by those 65 and older has grown, and 45% of them reported using social media (Faverio, 2022). Whereas marketing messages tailored for senior citizens are still delivered via the platforms of traditional media advertising and public relations, social media platforms and websites have emerged as go-to marketing channels. Since the senior market is easily identified by market segmentation, the mature, rich audience can be reached through email, websites and social media, mainly Facebook.

According to Pew Research, 13% of people over the age of 65 use Instagram, 49% use YouTube and 50% use Facebook (Auxier & Anderson, 2021). They are 19% more likely to share content than any other generation, and 58% more likely than millennials to click through to a brand's website from a social media post (Costa, 2021). Considering only Baby Boomers, they like to shop online as much as younger generations and use social media and websites to research products more than shop at brick-and-mortar stores, according to Candidsky (2021), a digital agency. Post COVID-19, these 56- to 74-year-olds have become, more than the average person might think, tech savvy and plugged into social media; indeed, this digital transformation accelerated almost overnight (Balis, 2021; Kis, 2021). The onset of the pandemic literally changed the online landscape for U.S. senior citizens, who use Facebook to keep in touch with friends and family, do online shopping and use Google to search for information on their laptops/PCs.

Marketing professional and business consulting agencies are offering their expertise after the United States has had two years of COVID-19 in senior marketing strategies in terms of distributing messages. Not surprisingly, they recommend banking on digital media channels such as websites, Facebook and YouTube to have marketing messages delivered to senior citizens, while not ignoring television commercials and direct mail (Batchelor, 2022; Page, 2022; Smith, 2022). What such experts emphasize is that marketing messages targeting senior citizens should first be crafted from attitudinal and behavioral insights to drive engagement with them, and then the messages need to be sent through proper channels in written form as well as video format as more senior

Box 6.2. The PESO Model

Gini Dietrich, author of *Spin Sucks*, told *PR Week*: "If you aren't using the PESO model for your communications work" (Thabit, 2015), you should be. The term *PESO* (Paid, Earned, Shared and Owned) represents a marketing and public relations strategy that promotes the integration of all possible media channels to deliver integrated marketing programs and messages to target audiences. The model, in parallel with the rapid growth of digital technology and social media, illustrates a convergence of integrated marketing practices of how to use traditional and social media to extend reach and establish brands (Xie, Neill & Schauster, 2018). Since senior citizens over 65 expressed and demonstrated their desire to learn and practice the new normal of digital communication, facing the world's predictable unpredictability—a new feasible living pattern for the rest of the 2020s with the pandemic—marketers and brands need to expedite the process of incorporating the PESO model into their marketing tactics for the senior citizen segment.

The PESO model, evolving from the earlier categorization of media content as "paid, owned and earned" was completed with a fourth component of shared media: social media (McNamara et al., 2016). Based on scholarly research (Pieczka, 2019; Wolf & Archer, 2018, we can apply the PESO model to the senior citizen segment as follows:

Paid media refers to traditional advertising and other forms of content commercially contracted between organizations and mass media, including television, newspapers, radio and magazines. These have been the dominant form of promotional media content for the past century, and senior citizens still feel comfortable in viewing and reading advertorial content via paid media.

Earned media is directly associated with the practice of having organizational messages published by the media or journalists. Media relations serves as the key function of earned media to create free but trustworthy publicity for organizations through press releases, interviews and promotional events. As senior citizens tend to trust journalists and news outlets more than other generations, earned media is a great way of promoting organizational images and reputations.

Shared media is another word for organic social media built on digital forums that social media users follow, commenting and expressing their opinions, including liking, disliking, thumbs up and down etcetera. Given the rise in popularity of social media among senior citizens, shared media is where organizations need to place more resources for the senior citizen segment by encouraging the generation to be part of the conversation and interact with their brands.

Owned media, including blogs, podcasts and websites, are created, organized and controlled by organizations that own such publishing platforms. Unlike shared media, owned media allows organizations to control what messages and media content they intend to distribute to the target audience. Since seniors have an increased level of overall use and savviness when it comes to technology, with 75% using the internet in 2020, organizations should keep refreshing their online content tailored for the senior citizen segment.

citizens prefer to view online videos that give clear how-to tips and what-to-buy information.

More importantly, the world has witnessed the popularity of short-form videos explode and social media platforms, in particular TikTok, go video-first. Short, fun and informative videos on social media should definitely be considered both a format and a channel that emerge and become a hot commodity in effectively spreading messages to senior citizens.

Shared and owned media can be the future or even present for organizations to target the senior market segment. However, they should not ignore the traditional paid and earned media since roughly two-thirds of adults 75 and older fall into the group having lower tech readiness, and half of Americans ages 65 to 74 expressed concern about their inability to use new digital devices, according to a 2021 Pew Research study (Faverio, 2022). In other words, the senior market segment is uniquely broad, comprehensive and rich from a PESO model perspective (see Box 6.2). All kinds of media strategies, tactics, outlets and platforms should be incorporated to inform, educate and entertain senior citizens in pursuit of marketing to the wealthy generation.

Entertaining Messages

Appendix B lists a selection of films over the last 50 years that depict senior citizens. Taylor (2012) writes that "Hollywood movies mostly ignore the old—or consign them to the demeaning Siberia of crazy old coots (Jack Nicholson) or wacky broads"; Taylor notes that the British call these films "wrinklies." Jack Nicholson, then 66, does star in one film on the list, "Something's Gotta Give" (2003), which costarred Diane Keaton, then 57. Nicholson's character could be called crazy, given his penchant for chasing much younger women, including the Keaton character's daughter. However, rather than deserving the blanket epithet "demeaning," many films on the list gained critical acclaim. *On Golden Pond* (1981), for example, won the Golden Globe for Best Picture-Drama; Henry Fonda, then 76, won the best actor Oscar for the film, and costar Katherine Hepburn, then 74, won the best actress Oscar.

Films even earlier than those on the list likewise sent positive messages. For example, in the first film to use Technicolor, *The Wizard of Oz* (1939), Dorothy (Judy Garland) went to Kansas to live with an older couple, Aunt Em and Uncle Henry (Dorothy's mother had died and her father had abandoned her). Em and Henry's portrayal was hardly "demeaning."

Appendix B also lists TV and streaming comedy/dramas. Young readers might assume that *Grace and Frankie* ushered in an era of successful comedy/dramas because the large cohort of Boomers (born 1946–1964) like seeing

Box 6.3. The Enduring Appeal
of *The Golden Girls*

Matt Browning, who received his BA in communications from West Virginia State University in 2004, may seem a bit youthful to be an uber fan of *The Golden Girls*, which aired 1985–1992. His passion resulted in a 400-page book, *The Definitive Golden Girls Cultural Reference Guide* (2021).

"I watched the show as a kid, with my mom and grandma," he explained (personal communication, May 28, 2022). "The book was my COVID project."

Browning, who manages the marketing and branding of WVSU's research program and extension service, publicized his book at the first Golden-con fan convention in Chicago, April 22–24, 2022—attended by "3,000-plus women and gay men."

The 180-episode series, which garnered 68 Emmy nominations, continues to "gain momentum with new, younger viewers" due to its "biting observations and timeless humor about issues" (Browning, 2021, p. v). Owned by Disney, the series currently airs on Hulu.

Browning, who owns the show's complete set of DVDs, says "timeless, universal values" helped make the show a hit, coupled with discussion of specific issues, such as elder care and the first time menopause was discussed on TV. In addition, "the writing, since even accomplished stars need a good script" and "the chemistry and balance of the cast, who were like the four points of a compass" were crucial.

Betty White, who died December 31, 2021, just a few weeks shy of her 100th birthday, complemented the ensemble cast of four single seniors who live together in Miami: Bea Arthur (1922–2009), the tallest, at 5-10; Estelle Getty (1923–2008), the petite one, at 4-11, who played Bea Arthur's mother but was actually younger than Arthur; and Rue McClanahan (1934–2010), the Southern man-crazy one, who in real life had six husbands.

characters depicted by stars their own age. However, the stars of *Grace and Frankie* actually fall into the category of "old old," rather than Boomer old; Jane Fonda (Grace) was born in 1937; Lily Tomlin (Frankie), 1939; Sam Waterston (Sol, Frankie's former husband), 1940; and Martin Sheen (Robert, Grace's former husband), 1940. The show's seven-season run shows that a "wrinklie" can succeed.

Moreover, in the pre-streaming era, *The Golden Girls* also ran for seven seasons (see Box 6.3). Now in the streaming era, it has added new fans to its already existing base of viewers from its original 1985–1992 run.

Chapter 6. Projects and Exercises

1. For *AARP The Magazine*, the largest U.S. magazine in circulation, analyze the editorial content for message themes. Do they reflect the organization's mission statement?
2. Find several people who have taken Road Scholar tours. Ask if particular words or messages attracted them.
3. Look at the messages of Viagra's competitors. Analyze the differences of these similar products.
4. Explore product ads targeting senior citizens—print or online—that appeared during the COVID-19 pandemic; discuss any differences in the same or similar product ads that appeared before the 2020 pandemic.
5. Visit several websites and social media platforms dealing with services (e.g., those listed in Box 1.1) for senior citizens. Which ones stand out and why from a marketing perspective?

CHAPTER 7

United States, Land of Retiree Options

Florida, the U.S. state with the largest net in-migration of people over 65 (see chapter 2), boasts not only Disney World in Orlando, but a Disney World for grownups outside of Orlando. The Villages, the largest master-planned city in the United States, should be understood "not as a town but as a peopled golf-delivery landscape" (Dudley, 2016, para 4). Called "TV" by its 130,000-plus residents—98.2% of them white—The Villages has 693 holes for golf, accessed by 65,000 golf carts.

Those under age 19 can visit the city, which started in the 1980s, for no more than 30 days a year. Without grandchild baby-sitting duties, residents can indulge in a party every night after golfing all day. Inevitably, the "TV" phenomenon attracted the lens of a documentary film maker (see Box 7.1.) Jimmy Buffett also chose Florida as the location for two of his Margaritaville 55-plus communities (see Box 7.2).

After Florida, Arizona has the second-highest in-migration of people over 65, so not surprisingly, age-specific retirement communities started there. Sun City, opened in 1960, spawned a spate of other communities. Its developer, Del Webb, even appeared on the cover of *Time* in 1962. Today Del Webb Active Adult Communities exist in 19 states. Leisure World, another chain, has seven locations that one can visit virtually.

North Carolina ranks as the third-largest U.S. retirement state, after Florida and Arizona. By 2034, the total economic impact in North Carolina of only one kind of retirement venue, Continuing Care Retirement Communities, is projected to be $3.2 billion (Appold, Johnson & Parnell, 2015).

In 2013, *The Journal of the Economics of Ageing* was established to deal with this interaction between economies and demographic changes. Living arrangements in their final—perhaps as long as 30—years of life will affect not only seniors themselves but also society at large in these three and other states.

Box 7.1. Media Images: Retirement Communities

Youthful Lance Oppenheimer, in his directorial debut, made an insightful documentary about older people. *Some Kind of Heaven* premiered at the Sundance Film Festival in 2020 and on streaming services in 2021. The documentary depicts a year in the lives of three residents and one quasi-resident of The Villages, a 55-plus retirement community outside of Orlando, FL.

The film "pierces the bubble" of a Disney World elder world near the actual Disney World, designed "for people who have cocooned themselves from the outside world" (Kenigsberg, 2021). As home to 130,000 residents, The Villages grew, between the 2010 and 2020 census, at the fastest pace of all U.S. metro areas (Burch, 2021).

While focusing on residents, some glimpses of Villages marketing are shown. In order to sell homes, founder Howard Schwartz, who expanded the complex from a venue that had only 800 residents in the mid-1980s, created the look of a small town that Boomers would find familiar. In addition to a brief look back to the 1980s, the documentary showed marketing in action, as a present-day, prospective-resident couple took a tour of an available home with a salesman.

Beyond the documentary, the heavily Trump-supporting Villages had an unrelated media presence when, in April 2022, two male residents pleaded guilty to voter fraud. One voted in Florida as well as, by absentee ballot, in Michigan; the other voted in Florida and Connecticut. Voter fraud, a third-degree felony, did not result in prison time, but in community service and attendance at an adult civics class with a grade of at least C–. While Donald Trump "continues to make false claims [about] widespread voter fraud" in Joe Biden's favor (Scott, 2022), the men actually convicted of fraud may have voted for Trump.

While the Oppenheimer documentary depicted a real venue, a fictional retirement venue was the subject of a 2021 Netflix dark comedy. In *I Care a Lot*, the manager of Berkshire Oaks, a high-end assisted-living care home, shows prospective residents the amenities of his facility. To prey on the elderly, the home's manager works with corrupt guardianship scammer Marla Grayson (Rosamund Pike, who won a best actress Golden Globe for the role). A reviewer (Lemire, 2021) remarked that "the grift is impressive," whereby legal loopholes in guardianship of the elderly permit an "operation [that] is at once stunning and terrifying." Over the first weekend of its February 19, 2021, release, "*I Care a Lot*" was the most-watched film on Netflix (Brueggemann, 2021). In real life, a marketing staff member rather than the home's manager likely would conduct tours of such a facility, but the film had to show complicity between Grayson and the facility's manager to move the plot along.

Box 7.2.   Jimmy Buffett's Margaritaville Brand

The approach of "turning emotions into a lifestyle brand" (Colapinto, 2021, p. 50) has worked wonders for Jimmy Buffett, 74. The performer himself originated the marketing phrase, "Where is Margaritaville? It's in your mind." In reality, his three Margaritaville retirement villages exist in solidly grounded locations: Daytona Beach and Panama Beach in Florida, as well as Hilton Head in South Carolina. Buffett's 1977 song "Margaritaville" has somewhat improbably morphed into a branding operation with more than $1 billion in sales annually.

In 1999, Buffett began working with John Cohlan, a Wall Street executive. As Cohlan told *AARP The Magazine*, he had seen 100,000 Buffett fans (called Parrot Heads) screaming ecstatically. Cohlan saw that fandom "'was really something emotional.' And emotion drives a brand" (Colapinto, 2021, p. 50).

The Daytona Beach location, built by Minto real estate development but branded by Margaritaville Holdings LLC, opened its sales center in 2017. The children born in 1949, the year with the highest number of Boomer births, reached retirement age in 2014; just about then, they may have started to think about relocating, and Buffett presented as an option his "'60s-infected sense of community . . . [with] the pursuit of fun . . . a powerful lure" (Colapinto, 2021, p. 50). Although the Margaritaville marketing materials use the phrase "Growing older but not up," one's retirement income needs to be comfortably up to afford the mid-$200,000 to mid-$400,000 base home price.

Marketing Messages

The myriad array of retirement options can make decision-making daunting, especially since cognitive decline can make such choices difficult for the elderly compared to younger people (Chen & Ma, 2009). Marketing aims to ease that choice, hoping to evoke a phone call or online reply indicating a person's interest, followed by a personal visit, paying an initial fee and ultimately, moving in. Settling on a specific type of retirement venue, if partly influenced by marketing materials, means that "how LTC [long-term care] facilities market their services is a critical matter" (Baiocchi-Wagner, 2012, p. 364).

This chapter will explore the nature of those materials' messages, which can tell us about the perceived values related to aging in U.S. society. What is emphasized and what is deemphasized? Does a mismatch exist between "fantasy" portrayals of aging and seniors' real-life experiences?

On the one hand, marketers may want to project an idyllic picture of their specific facility. On the other hand, if marketing messages misrepresent the facility, the disconnect that a prospective resident notices during an on-site visit risks eroding credibility. That dilemma will inform this chapter's analysis of images of aging.

Senior-Living Models

Various housing models for seniors exist. Bookman (2008) looked at three alternatives to "age-segregated retirement communities" (p. 419): (1) naturally occurring retirement communities (NORCs); (2) campus-affiliated communities; and (3) Villages (groups of members who own, and want to stay in, their homes). She used interviews and site visits to identify positive practices as well as problems, such as how to integrate low- and moderate-income seniors and minority seniors (in terms of language, race and culture) into aging-in-place retirement models. Fee-based condo complexes featuring smaller units, with mowing, snow removal and yard care provided, attract but don't necessarily limit ownership to those over 55. The Village model (Scharlach, Graham & Lehning, 2011) enables seniors to stay in their own homes—that is, aging in place; the authors received completed surveys from 30 of 42 fully functioning Villages. Funding, based solely on member fees and donations, will likely present future problems. Members help each other as well as make use of local agencies. Guo and Castillo (2012) argue for "formal and informal home and community-based services and support" (p. 210) in the form of NORCs.

Medicare's website has a "nursing home comparison tool" that lists certified Medicaid and Medicare facilities (Baiocchi-Wagner, 2012). The list includes high- and low-quality, as well as for-profit and not-for-profit, venues. Chapter 2 profiled SilverComm professionals who market nursing home and assisted living options. Medicare does not cover nursing home services—already costly and rising—for the fastest-growing senior segment, those 85 and older. Medicaid pays for low-income persons, but the middle- and higher-income elderly need other options; CCRCs can fill that need.

CCRCs, also known as life-care communities, provide—for those who can afford to live in the available apartments or houses—lifestyle amenities as well as health care facilities. Many are nonprofit and church affiliated. Chapter 3 profiled how SilverComm professionals at six CCRCs coped with the challenges of COVID. CCRCs provide three levels of lifelong care, usually all on one campus: independent living in a house or apartment, assisted living and skilled nursing. Residents can move from one level to another as their needs change (Hangley, 2022). They typically require a large entry fee, followed by a monthly fee (which includes housing and often meals, depending on the plan a resident chooses).

Senior-Living Studies

The reasons for moving to a continuing care retirement community include push factors such as a "desire to plan while still able to do so; optimal timing and being ready for a change; fear of burdening family; burden of home and yard maintenance; own or spouse's failing health; and environmental barriers" and pull factors including "attachment to the community; joining friends and neighbors who were moving at the same time; proximity to family; amenities of the CCRC and the prospect of long-term care in the future" as well as looking "forward to a new and exciting phase of life" (Groger & Kinney, 2006, pp. 79–80).

Marx et al. (2011), who surveyed 300 CCRC residents over five years, found that the main reason they moved was avoidance of home upkeep (48%); anticipating future needs ranked second (25.7%). By far, the residents (97.1%) were glad they moved, freed from worries, and gaining fulfilling social life/activities. Space constraints, especially in apartments, and multiple regulations were disadvantages. By year 5, the population of CCRCs was 68% female. In a smaller, earlier study, Krout et al. (2002) surveyed 91 older adults in the early 1990s in upstate New York regarding their reasons for moving to a CCRC.

In a rare senior-living marketing study, Baiocchi-Wagner (2012) did research on brochures from 56 randomly selected long-term care facilities. In Phase 1, a qualitative content analysis, she discerned four themes: importance of physical surroundings (especially an emphasis on nature); homogeneity of residents; health and happiness; and social capital. Phase 2 (quantitative) yielded results from 202 photographs that can be compared with the CCRC study in this chapter.

CCRC Website Marketing

This book's first author and a colleague (Ji & Cooper, 2017) analyzed websites of 108 U.S. CCRCs accredited by CARF (Commission on Accreditation of Rehabilitation Facilities) International, an "independent, nonprofit accreditor of health and human services" (CARF, n.d.). Often "visiting a facility is not a practical option (e.g., time and/or geographical constraints" (Baiocchi-Wagner, 2012, p. 353), so websites serve a key informational function.

The CARF list, a small portion of all CCRCs, are arguably the crème de la crème. Because of the organization's high standards, only the 216 CARF-accredited CCRCs listed on its own website as of December 15, 2016, were considered. The authors reduced the sample by half, selecting every other CCRC from a random starting point. The next four paragraphs come from Ji and Cooper (2017), with the permission of the first author.

PROCEDURES

Coding was done February 11–16, 2017. The unit of analysis was the image of a CCRC resident. Research (Yoon, Cole & Lee, 2009) shows that seniors respond to visuals more strongly than to print. For all ages, pictures make more of an impression than the proverbial 1,000 words (Hill, 2004; Paivio & Csapo, 1973). Slideshows, a popular website design approach, enable organizations to "showcase their work in a more interactive way" (Cronin, 2009, para. 6) than still photos. Also, the moving slides let visitors to the website quickly learn about a particular CCRC as they comb through many retirement facility options.

To collect the images, the authors developed a multistep protocol. *First*, using the website address as listed by CARF, the authors located each CCRC's home page. *Second*, residents' images were identified on the facility's home page. From a pretest, the authors observed that most CCRCs had slideshows. For those that did not, the authors coded the video entry photo to preserve the focus on visuals; by analogy, the entry photo serves as the cover of a magazine. Similarly, to focus consistently on visuals: if the website had neither a slideshow nor video, the dominant stand-alone photo was coded.

If a website slideshow had no residents (e.g., showed only interior and exterior shots of buildings), the coding process ended. Likewise, if a website had no slideshow at all, no video photo of a resident and no dominant photo with a resident, the coding ended. Of the 108 selected CCRC sites, 37 were omitted for those reasons and two sites disappeared between December 2016 to February 2017. Photos that showed only hands or torsos were not coded. For each photo, a maximum of four residents were coded (left to right) to avoid oversampling one visual.

THEORY: MASLOW'S HIERARCHY OF NEEDS

The classic typology developed by Maslow (1954), a humanist psychologist, described five needs that people must satisfy before they move to fulfilling the next level: (1) *physiological*—oxygen, food, water; (2) *safety*—security and protection; (3) *social*—love (both giving and receiving), affection, belongingness (absence of loneliness); (4) *esteem*—a high level of respect (absence of feeling weak, inferior, helpless and worthless); (5) *self-actualization*—realization of one's potential, with joyful feelings that life is worth living. Trying to actually meet all these needs would constitute an ambitious, perhaps unrealistic, goal for CCRCs, but no "law" prevents marketers from presenting an idealized version of senior living—up to and including Maslow's level 5.

FINDINGS

1.How many total CCRC residents are shown in CCRC websites?

Analysis of 108 CCRC websites, reduced to 69 that met the selection criteria, yielded 199 slideshow photos picturing 407 residents (a maximum of four persons per photo).

2.What percent of CCRC residents depicted are shown indoors and outdoors?

This study's CCRC residents were located about evenly indoors (45.5%, n = 185) and outdoors (47.7%, n = 194); other/can't tell was 6.9% (n = 28).

3. What percent of CCRC residents are shown alone and with others?

Of the CCRC residents pictured, only 14.0% (n = 57) were shown alone, with 86.0% (n = 350) of residents shown with others (see Figures 7.1, 7.2). The

There's so much to see at Brandon Wilde.

Get a closer look at all the friendly faces and fun activities at Brandon Wilde. Then fill out the form to come see it for yourself.

Eating Wilde   Home of the Wilde

Figure 7.1. The website for one Continuing Care Retirement Community (CCRC) includes this image of residents engaged in the most prevalent category of CCRC visuals: scenes of eating/drinking.

Media Gallery

Piedmont Gardens › About Us › Piedmont Gardens - Media Gallery

Photos   Videos   Virtual Tour

Photos

Our Community [32]

Our Lifestyle (35)

Our Residences [25]

Our Memory Care Community (10)

Our Life Plan Community offers all-inclusive living with a variety of floor plans and fees suitable for many budgets.

LEARN ABOUT PRICING

Figure 7.2. Like 86% of visuals showing CCRC residents, this image shows people with others, not alone. An unexpected finding revealed dogs as the pet of choice; no cats were pictured.

Community gardens are available as well

Figure 7.3. This CCRC website image exemplifies positive affect. In an extensive study of CCRC images, not one person was shown sad or frowning.

finding relates to level 3 of Maslow's (1954) hierarchy of needs, social, which encompasses an absence of loneliness. Though likely not intentionally referring to Maslow, intuitively the website designers wanted to convey a sense of belongingness that residents would experience if they moved to the CCRC.

4. How do the CCRC residents relate to others?

The majority (54.3%) of residents were pictured with at least two other residents, while more than a quarter (25.7%) were shown with a resident of the opposite gender plus 4.3% with visitor(s). The CCRC world brims with a rich social life, complemented by moments with one's significant other. This picture of affection and belongingness again confirms Maslow's (1954) level 3. Results also affirm Maslow's level 4, esteem—absence of feeling weak and helpless; only seven of 350 individuals are shown getting help from staff. CCRCs typically include many independent living units, so most residents do not need extreme amounts of help from staff. However, the CCRCs themselves must have decided not to emphasize a "nursing home aura" in their marketing materials.

5. What percent of residents exhibit positive/happy, negative/sad and neutral affect?

Maslow's (1954) level 5—a joyful feeling that life is worth living—characterizes residents depicted in promotional materials for the varied types of senior living on which the two studies focused. This result produced the most striking commonality between the two marketing studies: the total absence of negative/sad residents. Baiocchi-Wagner's (2012) people pictured in brochures were 85.7% positive/happy and 14.3% neutral. The website research coded 75.2% (n = 306) of people as positive/happy; 10.8% (n = 44) as neutral; and 14.0% (n = 57) as other/can't tell. (See Figure 7.3.)

6. What percent of residents are engaged in active fulfilling, semi-active fulfilling and non-fulfilling pursuits?

Table 7.1 shows a wondrous array of fulfilling pursuits, although of course without objective measures of the satisfaction these activities bring. Taken together, the websites illustrate Maslow's (1954) level 5, self-actualization, and level 4, esteem—an absence of feeling inferior and helpless. One can almost hear the residents saying, "There are simply not enough hours in the day!"

Given that dining/eating/drinking (see Table 7.1) was by far the top activity at 23.1%, the social aspect of this activity visualizes Maslow's level 3, social. Table 7.1 gives detailed descriptions of other activities, including sitting (9.6%),

Table 7.1.   Residents' Activities—CCRC Websites

Type of Interactions	Frequency	Percent
Active		
Walking	32	7.9
Hiking	17	4.2
Swimming	13	3.2
Biking	12	2.9
Dancing	10	2.5
Gardening	9	2.2
Boating/kayaking	5	1.2
Golfing	4	1.0
Jogging	2	0.9
Woodworking	2	0.5
Other active	11	2.7
Subtotal	117	28.7
Semi-active		
Eating/drinking	94	23.1
Sitting	39	9.6
Standing	22	5.4
Reading	17	4.2
Gazing	9	2.2
Painting	8	2.0
Hugging	8	2.0
Watching a show	4	1.0
Bird watching	4	1.0
Cooking	4	1.0
Playing cards/game	3	0.7
Riding in a vehicle	2	0.5
Learning in class	2	0.5
Teaching	1	0.2
Working at computer	1	0.2
Yoga/mat work	1	0.2
Other/semi-active	20	4.9
Subtotal	239	58.7
Other/can't tell	13	3.2
Head shot	38	9.3
TOTAL	407	100

Source: Ji and Cooper (2017)

head shots (9.3%) and walking (7.9%). CCRC results showed fewer active 28.7% (n = 117) than semi-active 58.7% (n = 239) pursuits, with other/can't tell at 3.2% (n = 13) and head shots at 9.3% (n=38).

7. What percent of CCRC photos show residents with infirmities vs. what are the actual percentages of CCRC residents with infirmities?

Of the CCRC residents, 99.5% (n = 405) have no visible infirmity; photos showed only 0.2% (one resident with a cane) and 0.2% (one resident with a walker). No one was shown in a hospital bed.

In actuality, anyone who enters a CCRC immediately notices walkers, wheelchairs, scooters and canes. Given the average age of 85 in at least one facility and the fact that centenarians live at virtually every CCRC, a high level of infirmity would be expected. However, the depiction of sickness does not jive with the fantasy world of self-actualized, happy seniors enjoying their golden years. As Baiocchi-Wagner (2012, p. 361–362) states, although the absence of infirm residents "may do much good for brochure readers, there is a great potential for a negative expectancy violation."

DISCUSSION AND CONCLUSIONS

This study of 407 photos from 69 randomly selected, accredited U.S. CCRC websites showed residents depicted as happily enjoying the company of others, pursuing a variety of fulfilling activities (especially wining and dining), while enjoying good health—free of wheelchairs, walkers and canes. Baiocchi-Wagner's (2012) charge of "intentional deceit to a certain degree" (p. 363) may be true. The common marketing strategy, judging from websites, is promoting companionships and belongingness; the elderly can expect healthy and happy lives if they move to these facilities.

Maslow's (1954) highest level, level 5, self-actualization; level 4, esteem needs; and level 3, social needs—all were confirmed as prominent on website visuals; moreover, level 1, physiological needs, as well as level 2, safety, were implied in the photos as well. The more self-actualized and socially satisfied residents appeared to be, the more did the negative aspects of aging seem ignored.

Enlightened self-interest would seem to argue for accurate depictions, but such was not the case. A disconnect between reality and website visuals occurs on several levels, bringing into question the CCRCs' credibility as a source (Hovland & Weiss, 1951). In the "website world," residents with infirmities were underrepresented, compared to the real world.

One reason for this deck stacking could be the pressure to "deliver" new residents, since some staff make cold sales calls and work on commission. One marketing director, who has served in her position for 23 years, said in an email that recently "the field has become much more competitive," increasing the importance of promotional materials.

Niche design firms that specialize in senior-oriented visuals and websites can spend hours with a CCRC staff, board of directors and residents before even beginning the site creation process (G. Likins, personal communication, March 23, 2022). The design team might use multiple cameras to record visuals, plus a videographer—taking care to choose which shade of lightbulb looks best and which chair sets the desired mood.

Despite the care lavished on websites, they have limitations. For a couple wishing to move to a CCRC in the South from, say, a rust-belt city, websites can indeed help narrow their search. However, one typical CCRC draws about two-thirds of its residents—who wanted to stay where they already lived—from the immediate area. Other locals making similar retirement choices no doubt never even look at websites. Finally, in coding the 407 photos, the authors noticed the presence of many dogs—appearing in scenes of residents walking outdoors, as well as sitting inside—but not one cat. Future research might delve into this pet-preference phenomenon.

Chapter 7. Projects and Exercises

1. Duplicate the method in this chapter for website images of retirement communities near you.
2. Locate a website design firm that, ideally, designs senior living websites. Interview the designers about their process, from initial interviews with CEO and staff to choice of visuals and copy in creating the final product.
3. Visit an over-55 retirement community. How would you design its marketing materials?
4. Find one single male and one single female senior who live in a retirement community (not necessarily the same one); guide them through signing up for a dating app such as Silver Singles and OurTime.
5. Make a YouTube or TikTok video that sheds light on self-actualization of senior citizens by focusing on their peaceful minds derived from their specific activities and mindsets toward life.

Part IV

CURRENT ISSUES

CHAPTER 8

Gender, Race and Sexual Orientation

In Episode 3, Season 1 of *Grace and Frankie*, Jane Fonda and Lily Tomlin try desperately to get the attention of a store clerk, who can't take his eyes off a 20ish female customer in a low-cut tank top. When Grace and Frankie finally leave the store in a huff, an exasperated Grace says, "I refuse to be irrelevant!" Whereupon Frankie, who comically used her invisibility, shows Grace the shoplifted item that the two were trying to buy.

As if Netflix's comedy art had imitated life, Pat Moore (1986) likewise experienced invisibility and indifference; although actually only 26, she disguised herself for three years as an 85-year-old woman. While repeating parts of Moore's experiment, Sheila Green (1991), a nurse, got similar reactions. Another woman, who used to have to contend with leering gazes, now "often feels as though she recedes into the background and is overlooked by wait staff, salespeople and others" (Tretheway, 2001, p. 201). More recently, Busch (2019) authored an *Atlantic* article titled "The Invisibility of Older Women."

These real and fictional stories illustrate how older women may enter a marginalized state—unseen, unheard—exacerbated by women's loss of height, more pronounced than men's, of about three inches by age 80. Images can also convey marginalization (Sherman, 1997).

This chapter explores erasure. How do "products of popular culture . . . impart information about our gendered and racial identities" (Johnson, Richmond & Kivel, 2008, p. 303) as we age?—specifically, advertising and marketing-oriented websites. Who experiences erasure by these persuasive media? Why?

The chapter also looks at gender issues in the SilverComm professions, as well as aging challenges that gay men and lesbian women face. When we look at the intersection of age, gender, race and sexual orientation, we see the beginning of what this book's authors call elderist theory. Elderist theory

Box 8.1. Context Data: U.S. Demographics

The U.S. Census Bureau (2020) has reported that in 2019, there were 4.942 million more elder females than males in the age group of 65 and over. Not surprisingly, more elders fall into the "young old" category than older cohorts (men aged 65–69, 4.5% of all males; women, 4.7% of all females).

Census data estimates for 2020 of the total U.S. population (all ages) of 331,449,281 have the percentage breakdowns as follows: White, 76.3% (not Hispanic, 60.1%); Black, 13.4%; Asian, 5.9%; Hispanic, 18.5%; two or more races, 2.8%. Persons 65 and over totaled 16.5%.

As Arber and Ginn (1991, p. 9) point out, there were "more elderly men than women in the population until 1930. Since then there has been a steep rise in the sex ratio, reaching 46 percent more elderly women than men in the late 1980s." About 75 percent of U.S. elderly men are married, versus 40 percent of elderly women. Due to greater life expectancy, women have a higher probability of widowhood than men of the same age. As Chambers (2000, p. 127) states, widowhood is "the *likely* circumstance of older women . . . the norm as they move into old, old age."

posits that media portrayals of elders, while evolving over time, do not replicate elders' actual demographics (see Box 8.1); women and minorities are especially underrepresented.

Ageisim, Sexism and Racism

As Tretheway (2001, p. 185) states, "Age ideology has not been theorized by communication scholars, yet it is probably as important as gendered or racial ideologies in terms of influencing our individual and collective experiences and our identities." Tretheway further states that older women "face the double blow of sexism and ageism" (184). A subfield emerged when some sociologists (e.g., Arber & Ginn, 1991; Bernard et al., 2000; Calasanti & Slevin, 2001; Krekula, 2007) incorporated the 1960s concept of ageism (Butler, 1969) into the context of women's studies. Calasanti and Slevin (2001, p. 3) wrote their book *Gender, Social Inequalities and Aging* because "feminist perspectives remain little used in gerontology."

Calasanti and Slevin (2001, p. 187) further assert that the concerns of feminists in the 1960s and 1970s with "reproductive rights inevitably led to a concentration on the lives of younger women." Indeed, a standard women's studies textbook (Kolman & Bartkowski, 2010) devotes less than one page to "older" women by reprinting the 1980 mission statement of the Older Women's League (OWL). However, aimed at women merely over 40, OWL addressed the concerns of married and divorced women with children. (OWL went out of existence at the national level in March 2017). The U.S. women's movement has been mostly associated with white, middle-class women.

Although no organization devoted solely to older Black, Hispanic, or Asian women seems to exist, three groups advocate for both male and female minority elders (see Appendix C). The National Asian Pacific Center on Aging, founded in 1979, helps Asian American elders overcome cultural, linguistic and economic obstacles. The National Hispanic Council on Aging, incorporated in Denver in 1980, has its headquarters in Washington, D.C., to advocate for the rapidly growing Hispanic elder population.

The National Caucus and Center on Black Aging, Inc. founded in 1970, has its headquarters in Washington, D.C. As its CEO Karyn Jones states, "You might see an ad featuring an older Black woman going to a pharmacy or acting as a caregiver, but you don't see images of older Black women buying luxury goods or exercising" (Dychtwald, 2021, p. 9).

What does the research say about gender, race and age as represented in advertising? Rather than a race, Hispanic or Latinx models represent an ethnic or language affinity, but many studies have included this diverse group in their analyses.

Advertising

GENDER PORTRAYALS, PRINT MEDIA

Gantz, Gartenberg and Rainbow (1980) found that 80% of the senior-citizen models were male (i.e., only 20% female). Cooper-Chen, Leung, and Cho (1994), who studied 12 issues of *Time* (one issue per month, randomly selected) as well as all monthly issues of *Cosmopolitan* and *Esquire* that were published in 1989, found similar female invisibility. Male models over age 50 in the U.S. magazines numbered 93 (7.8%), while female models numbered only 28 (2.4%) of 1,184 models (a more than 3 to 1 male/female ratio).

Likewise confirming other research, McConatha, Schell and McKenna (1999) looked at a total of 2,505 people in 765 ads in *Time* and *Newsweek* during one year. Older adults were shown infrequently, especially older women (Yanni, 1990). On the ironically named silver screen, at 22.3% of senior characters (Smith, Choueiti & Pieper, 2017), older women are even harder to find. Female invisibility has thus been well documented.

In 20 years of ads in *Time* magazine (Ji & Cooper, 2022, as described in detail in chapter 4), of 590 elder models, gender distortion stands out as the authors' most striking finding; *Time*'s elder models inhabit a world more than three-quarters (76.4%) male—quite contrary to the actual demographics: 4.942 million more elder females than males (U.S. Census Bureau, 2020). In 2019, women aged 60 and over made up 12.2% of the U.S. population, while men made up 10.4%. Thus, the (real) majority contrasts markedly, even shockingly, with the (portrayed) minority.

MINORITY PORTRAYALS

Regarding minorities, Bramlett-Solomon and Wilson (1989) looked at the years 1978–1987 in *Life* and *Ebony* to explore the aspect of race and the elderly. An update (Bramlett-Solomon & Subramanian, 1999), which looked at 9,314 ads 1990–1997, found that fewer seniors appeared than a decade earlier; only 0.9% of ads in *Life* and 1.3% of ads in *Ebony* showed elders. Further, the later ads depicted more association with products and services specifically for the elderly. Interestingly, a larger proportion of Black elderly appeared in *Life* than White elderly in *Ebony*.

Just after the focus period of the *Life/Ebony* study, Paek and Shah (2003) looked at ads in the year 2000. They found these percentages of ads with minorities in *Time*: Blacks, in 9.8% of ads; Asian Americans, in 5.6%; Latinx, in 4.8%. Germane to this chapter, their results (for three newsweeklies combined) included the age of their three focus groups' models: of all African Americans, 19.7% were old (retired); of all Latinx, 10.6% were old; and of all Asian Americans, 5.7% were old. Looked at another way, they found that African Americans represented the vast majority of elder minority models, 70%; Latinx, 19%; and Asian Americans, 11%. While Paek and Shah (2003, p. 233) did not report the gender of older minority models, they did find that, overall, "African American and Latino females were practically invisible." Lei, Cooper-Chen and Cheng (2007) looked at Asian elder portrayals (see chapter 4).

More recently, Ji and Cooper (2022) addressed key questions. Are White elders portrayed in *Time* ads proportional to their percent in the population? Are Black minority elders portrayed in *Time* ads proportional to their percent in the population? Are other minority elders portrayed in *Time* ads proportional to their percent in the population?

Table 8.1 gives varied answers to the three questions. For White elders, the findings range from a slight underrepresentation in 2000, to a slight overrepresentation in 2010, to a sizable overrepresentation in 2019 (17.3% in ads, but only 12.4% in reality).

Given Black elders' low actual percent in the population, any presence at all in the "ad world" can almost replicate reality; in fact, the 2019 ad population

Table 8.1.   Percent of White Elders, Black Elders and Asian Elders Portrayed in *Time* Ads vs. Percent of White Elders, Black Elders and Asian Elders in the U.S. Population over Time

	2000	2010	2019
% of White elders in *Time* ads	10.0	11.8	17.3
% of White elders in the U.S. population	10.4[a]	10.1[b]	12.4[c]
% of Black elders in *Time* ads	1.2	0.4	1.5
% of Black elders in the U.S. population	1.0[a]	1.1[b]	1.6[c]
% of Asian elders in *Time* ads	0.2	0.8	0
% of Asian elders in the U.S. population	0.3[a]	0.5[d]	0.8[e]

[a] Calculation for the percent of White, Black and Asian elders (aged 65 and over) in the U.S. population in 2000 is based on Census data from "Table 1. Total Population by Age, Race and Hispanic or Latino Origin for the United States: 2000." Retrieved on November 1, 2020, from https://www.census.gov/data/tables/2000/dec/phc-t-09.html. "White alone, not Hispanic" data were used.
[b] Calculation for the percent of White and Black elders (aged 65 and over) in the U.S. population in 2010 is based on Census data from "Table 1 Population by Sex and Age, for Black Alone and White Alone, Not Hispanic: 2010." Retrieved November 1, 2020, from https://www.census.gov/data/tables/2010/demo/race/ppl-ba10.html.
[c] Calculation for the percent of White and Black elders (aged 65 and over) in the U.S. population in 2019 is based on Census data from "Table 1. Population by Sex and Age, for Black Alone and White Alone, Not Hispanic: 2019." Retrieved November 1, 2020, from https://www.census.gov/data/tables/2019/demo/race/ppl-ba19.html.
[d] Calculation for the percent of Asian elders (aged 65 and over) in the U.S. population in 2010 is based on Census data from "Table 1. Population by Sex and Age, for Asian Alone or in Combination and White Alone, Not Hispanic: 2010." Retrieved on November 1, 2020, from https://www.census.gov/data/tables/2010/demo/race/ppl-ac10.html.
[e] Calculation for the percent of Asian elders (aged 65 and over) in the U.S. population in 2019 is based on Census data from "Table 1. Population by Sex and Age, for Asian Alone and White Alone, Not Hispanic: 2019." Retrieved on November 1, 2020, from https://www.census.gov/data/tables/2019/demo/race/ppl-aa19.html.
Source: Ji and Cooper (2022). Reprinted by permission of Taylor and Francis Ltd.

(1.5%) nearly matches the census figure of 1.6% (see Figure 4.2). For Asians, with both their actual (0.8% in 2019) and ad presence (0) so low, one should avoid drawing firm conclusions. Coders identified only one Hispanic elder model in *Time* ads.

RACE AND GENDER, 2020 AND 2021

The recent update created for this chapter exhibits a sea change in portrayals. Tables 8.2 and 8.3 show a presence of Black elders—especially men, but to some extent women—more than their actual percentage in the U.S. population. Considering Tables 8.2 and 8.3 together, one still sees underrepresentation of women overall (41.2% of models) vs. men (58.3% of models).

Table 8.2.   Seniors' Gender and Race in Advertisements, *Time*, 2020

	White	Black	Asian	Totals
Male	18	8	1	27 (50.9 %)
Female	17	8	1	26 (49.1 %)
TOTAL	35 (66%)	16 (30.2%)	2 (3.8%)	53 (100%)

Table 8.3.   Seniors' Gender and Race in Advertisements, *Time*, 2020

	White	Black	Asian	Hispanic	Totals
Male	17 (34%)	8 (16%)	7 (14%)	1 (2%)	33 (66.0%)
Female	13 (26%)	3 (6%)	0	1 (2%)	17 (34.0%)
TOTAL	30 (60%)	11 (22%)	7 (14%)	2 (4%)	50 (100%)

Note: The relatively large number of Asian men resulted from a series of institutional ads by Japanese and Korean sponsors.

IN RETROSPECT

Taken together, research shows evidence of elders' increasing presence in legacy media over time. Given their considerable wealth, the silver tsunami of aging Baby Boomers makes them hard to ignore. The invisibility in the 1970s of *all* elders prompted Gantz, Gartenberg and Rainbow (1980, p. 60) to state that they were "not considered to play a major role in the consumer society." However, even today female "residents" of the ad world still suffer erasure to some extent. Pointing to a possible reason, Dychtwald (2021) notes that 71% of the creative directors in the ad agency industry are male. Females' real and perceived lack of economic clout no doubt plays a role.

Given the lopsided portrayal of men over the years 2000–2019 (76% of models) versus 2020–2021 (58.3%), female elder models have indeed moved closer to older women's majority status in the real world. Elderist theory, based on these findings, holds that women as portrayed in ads still face partial erasure, but their numerical presence is improving. Ji and Cooper (2022) did not provide 20-year data specifically on older Black women (nor on Asian and Hispanic women), so the limited findings for 2020–2021 preclude any firm conclusions about progress.

Senior Housing Websites

As of December 31, 2019, market capitalization of U.S. senior housing and care facilities was estimated at $475 billion. COVID (see chapter 3) adversely affected occupancy, but analysts think it will have recovered to pre-COVID-19 levels by 2022 (Sudo, 2021). Full occupancy clearly affects the bottom line of both for-profit and not-for-profit facilities. For example, assisted living in a one-bedroom apartment with full kitchen at one Virginia location runs to $7,000 a month, while an efficiency apartment in Oregon runs to $5,000 a month (both with three meals a day).

Given these costs of senior housing, the standard financial criteria for entry would preclude low-income seniors from moving in. In 2019, Asian median household income, at $98,174, outpaced that of other ethnicities: Caucasian (not Hispanic), $76,057; Hispanic (any race), $56,113; and Black, $45,438 (Statista, 2022). How does the lower income of Black and Hispanic seniors relate to marketing images and practices?

As described in chapter 7, this book's first author and a colleague (Ji & Cooper, 2017) did the most extensive marketing-related analysis to date of senior housing visuals. They looked at websites of 108 U.S. Continuing Care Retirement Communities (CCRCs) accredited by the Commission on Accreditation of Rehabilitation Facilities (CARF), an "independent, nonprofit accreditor of health and human services" (CARF, n.d.). Often "visiting a facility is not a practical option," given time and geography constraints (Baiocchi-Wagner, 2012, p. 353), so websites serve a key informational function.

PORTRAYALS OF GENDER

Ji and Cooper (2017) found males to be 35.6% (n = 145); females, 62.7% (n = 255); and other/can't tell, 1.7% (n = 7). Baiocchi-Wagner (2012) coded residents as 55% female, 44% male. Both male percentages are unrealistically high.

Marx et al. (2011) found females to be 68% in their study of CCRC residents. Census data confirms that over-65 females far outnumber their male counterparts. One could speculate that single females—a larger prospective resident pool than single males—might find the depiction of men a positive aspect with some potential to affect their decision to visit a CCRC. Further, men might find the idea of male companions attractive.

The majority (54.3%) of residents were pictured with at least two other residents, while more than a quarter (25.7%) were shown with a resident of the opposite gender. The CCRC visual world brims with the rich social life of the retirement-as-resort model (Simpson & Cheney, 2007), complemented by moments with one's significant other.

Female–female dyads (see Figure 7.2) represent 7.4% of individuals—which seems low given the demographics of the actual over-65 female population.

Some widowed women move to CCRCs after their husbands die, while others lose their husbands after both move in. The plethora of single women at any CCRC makes female friendships inevitable; compared to older men, women have more same-sex networks (Adams, 1997).

Ji and Cooper (2019) found that about half (49.8%) of women are shown indoors—whether because of physical limitations or conforming to the stereotype that "women's place is in the home." By contrast, only 38.6% of men are shown indoors.

As chapter 7 noted, no residents at all were shown with negative affect (angry, crying, frowning, looking depressed). Interestingly, women (81.2% positive) looked far happier than men (68.3% positive).

Women (85.1%) and men (87.6%) are depicted with others at about the same rate. According to Adams (1997), older women do have more same-gender networks, same-age friends and more supportive relatives than do men. Overall, in the U.S. population, only 40% of older women are married (Arber & Ginn, 1991). Similarly, interactions underrepresented female friendships in the form of female–female dyads (7.4% of individuals), especially when compared to the high number of male–female dyads (25.7%).

PORTRAYALS OF RACE

Ji and Cooper (2017) found the CCRC photo population to be 89.4% White (n = 364); 5.2% (n = 21) Black; 2.0% (n = 8) Asian; and 3.4% (n = 14) other/can't tell. Baiocchi-Wagner's population was similar, 86.1% Caucasian, but higher, 10.3%, for African Americans; she also found 1.4% Hispanics, 1.1% Asians, 0.4% other and 0.7% indiscernible.

Among the eight total Asians in the CCRC sample, six were from Hawaii, one from Virginia, and one from Arizona. The 21 depicted Black residents were from nine states, including six from California, four from Connecticut, three from Pennsylvania, two each from Illinois and Nevada and one each from Washington, D.C., Massachusetts, Mississippi and Virginia. The study found two interracial couples—one from Hawaii (Asian woman/White man) and the other from Pennsylvania (Black woman/White man).

There is no way to tell if the minority elders pictured on websites actually live at the CCRC that their website depicts. The need to appear diverse clearly matters to some CCRCs, but how do SilverComm professionals deal with the dearth of minorities?

"Racially we're not where we need to be," stated Gretchen Likins, admissions/public relations director at Carol Woods, a CCRC in Chapel Hill, NC.

We don't use [professional] models in our materials, and [our few Black residents] are tired of being the model. We do use a Black board member in materials, as she is a part of CW. The board is diverse. We're working on it [making the resident population more diverse]. We sponsor the MLK Jr. banquet that the NAACP holds. To show our values, 95% of our ad budget goes to attracting diverse residents. It's illegal to ask about race [on an app form]. (personal communication March 23, 2022)

IMPLICATIONS: CCRC MARKETING PRACTICES

Marketing, which is "designed to generate interest in and attract prospects . . . is a priority in the management of a senior community" (Pearce, 2007, p. 181). No law is broken if CCRC promotional materials do not replicate the reality of residents. However, Baiocchi-Wagner (2012, p. 363) goes out on a limb by ascribing "intentional deceit to a certain degree" on the part of elder-targeted brochure creators. The Ji and Cooper (2017) study finds an issue of source credibility that does not rise to the level of deceit but that can be called distortion in the gender depictions on websites—possibly a surprising finding, given that women overwhelmingly dominate CCRC marketing staffs—however, the youthfulness of the staff, compared to the elderly female residents, could create a disconnect (Macdonald, 1983).

Communication researchers, beginning in the 1950s (Hovland & Weiss, 1951), have linked sources to message effectiveness. High-credibility sources usually persuade more effectively than low-credibility sources (see meta-analysis by Pornpitakpan, 2004). The complex process leading to attitude change, then beyond to behavior, can include 12 distinct steps (McGuire, 1989).

In the case of CCRC marketers, the hoped-for behaviors include a call or online reply indicating a person's interest, followed by a visit to the CCRC, then paying the "listing" fee and, ultimately, moving to the CCRC. If marketing messages misrepresent the facility, the disconnect that a prospective resident notices during an on-site visit risks moving the source from high-credibility to low-credibility status.

Along with multiple other factors, the diminished trust can affect attitudes and behavior. According to Werner and Mower (1986, p. 309), practitioners who wish to persuade "should carefully consider the extent which prospective target audiences perceive the level of bias and expertise of sources of information."

Consultants may influence clients to make CCRCs look more inviting by showing more racial diversity and more couples than actually live at a given facility. However, as Kotler and Armstrong (2014) stress, truthfulness best serves marketers. A reputation for deception once lost on the part of a business can only be recovered with difficulty. Thus, in the case of CCRC websites, enlightened self-interest could result in a more truthful race and gender picture.

Practitioners

A feminization-and-the-profession perspective can add another dimension to content analyses. A seminal article (Grunig, Toth & Hon, 2000) explores the parallels between ethical public relations practice and feminist values: cooperation, respect, caring, nurturance, interconnection, justice, equity, honesty, sensitivity, perceptiveness, intuition, altruism, fairness, morality and commitment. Moreover, in a newer book, Aldoory and Toth (2021) outline a feminist future for public relations and strategic communication.

Although anecdotal, the vast majority of professionals mentioned in chapter 2 are female: at Brightview Senior Living (4), The Village at Penn State (2), Road Scholar/Elderhostel (1), Hospice of Ohio (1), LeadingAge national headquarters (3) and AARP national headquarters (3). Furthermore, the seven communicators and/or marketers (whichever function was responsible for communication) at CCRCs who agreed to be interviewed for chapter 3 were female. They worked in six states: North Carolina, Pennsylvania, Ohio, Kansas, Colorado and Oregon.

Sexual Orientation and Aging

In terms of truthfulness, does the decision to portray same-sex couples on CCRC websites ever arise? Gretehen Likins of Carol Woods CCRC in North Carolina, stated that two residents were willing to be a part of the CCRC's website video as a couple and to be pictured together in a brochure. (They had gotten married in New York when same-sex marriage became legal there.) Profiles of new residents at Carol Woods in the community's newsletter openly mention if, for example, two female cohabitants are married.

"Marketing people [at other CCRCs] have told me, 'We have no gay residents.' I say to them, 'Yes, you do. You just don't know who they are.'" Carol Woods's proactive efforts include a presence at the Raleigh Gay Pride fest and the Out South film fest. "People want to know, 'Am I in a safe environment?' I have these rainbow pens [in my office]. The best marketing is to have residents bring gay friends here," Likins concluded. She knows of at least one case whereby someone discouraged a gay woman from moving into a particular community.

The LGBTQ older population was "once stereotyped as lonely, depressed, effeminate men preying on young boys, or cold, masculine women seducing young girls," but the current gerontological literature shows "a much different reality. Older gay men and lesbians are a diverse population, with many aging successfully" (Slusher, Mayer & Dunkle, 1996, p. 118).

Netflix viewers may not have previously thought about LGBTQ aging issues—until they saw *Grace and Frankie*, which depicted the romance and marriage of Sol and Robert, played by actors Sam Waterston, age 75 when the series debuted in 2015, and Martin Sheen, also age 75 in 2015. Nor would many have considered the question, Does the Fair Housing Act prohibit discrimination on the basis of sexual orientation? (It doesn't). Indeed, only 18% of long-term care facilities prohibit discrimination based on sexual orientation, while some refuse to accept LGBTQ women and men as residents, according to SAGE CEO Michael Adams (*PBS NewsHour Weekend*, 2021).

Diedra Nottingham, 69, interviewed on the same news feature, said that because staff at other residential facilities harassed her, she moved into Stonewall House, a 6,800 square-foot, 145-unit facility—New York State's first LGBTQ+ welcoming residence for those aged 62 and over. "I've been waiting 50 years" for a place like this, she said on the PBS broadcast. SAGE Center Brooklyn partners with Stonewall House, which opened in 2019. Tenants are mostly (77%) people of color, all earning 60% or less of the area's median income. It is 50% LGBTQ and 50% straight. Similar facilities already exist Los Angeles, Philadelphia and Minneapolis.

The SAGE (Services and Advocacy for Gay Elders) organization, founded in 1978 by Doug Kimmel, has its headquarters in Manhattan. (See Appendix C.) A separate organization, GLOW (Gays and Lesbians Older and Wiser) was a pioneering support group at a geriatric clinic at the University of Michigan in Ann Arbor (Slusher, Mayer & Dunkle, 1996).

Lest readers think older gay Americans dwell only on serious issues, they need only join the 7.1 million followers of the Four Old Gays on Tik Tok. These four senior men, who have been friends for 50 years, now live in Cathedral City, California. Starting in December 2020, they have been creating segments for the platform that may show them performing in regular clothes or underwear. They also have a few hundred thousand fans on Instagram (Locke, 2022).

Chapter 8. Projects and Exercises

1. Analyze any of the streaming/ cinema productions listed in Appendix B for their gender and race portrayals of older characters.
2. Use the method in chapter 4 to analyze the gender and race of models in *AARP The Magazine* for the most recent year or randomly selected years.

3. Visit a local CCRC to observe the gender ratio. Then compare this real-world data with that institution's website.

4. Follow female senior celebrities on Instagram such as Martha Stewart and Vera Wang, and apply content analysis to their photos and videos. From a sexism and ageism perspective, what did you find?

5. Explore online forums for senior citizens who are member of the LGBTQ community (see resources at choicemutual.com). What issues and concerns are discussed?

CHAPTER 9

What's Ahead?

"In countries aging the best, half of today's 10-year-olds may live to age 104," states Staci Jones-Alexander, AARP vice president, Thought Leadership (private webinar, January 22, 2022). "Our students should think about this population. There will be an increase in any job related to the aged, such as gerontologists." What will work look like in the future? "We know that we don't need to preserve legacy ways of doing things," Alexander concluded.

Future studies, an academic and business-oriented discipline (see Box 9.1), delves into issues, including the silver tsunami, that all of us should consider. The new gray reality will have myriad effects, both large and small. Increases in the geriatric population in the United States and other nations will drive a rise in a senior-oriented focus. At a personal level, products like washing machines must adjust to shorter physiques to accommodate seniors. At a societal level, from 1975 to 2008, consistently 3.2–3.4 workers existed for each retiree, but by 2034, the ratio will likely drop to 2.3–2 workers per retiree. In that year, the Social Security trust fund is expected to run out (de Rugy & Leventhal, 2018).

Beyond young people facing this bleak financial picture, another societal implication exists: increased automation. The lack of young workers relative to aging consumers means that robots or technological innovations will need to assist with or take over many jobs (BBC World Service, 2021a), so that the reduced work force can concentrate on other professions. Automation advances, coupled with an aging citizenry, will omit jobs such as truck driver (Stock, 2022). The United Nations (2019) estimated that, given the current 703 million persons aged 65 or over in the world, the number would double to 1.5 billion in 2050. The elder care market will grow a projected 7% every year from 2020 to 2027, reaching $2 trillion by 2027, according to a research institution specializing in global elderly analysis (Data Bridge Market Research, 2020).

Box 9.1. The Field of Future Studies: Institutes and Organizations

- World Future Society (www.worldfuture.org): Founded in 1966, the World Future Society is recognized as the largest, most influential and longest-running community of future thinkers in the world. The mission of World Future Society states: "Awaken the Futurist Mindset in everyone in order to co-create new civilization systems." It offers educational courses, including training for professionals, scholars and individuals who must sign up for membership that costs either $9.99 per month to join and participate in forums or $29.99 to have access to a special program for futurists. Only members are allowed to join and access future education courses.
- International Institute of Forecasters (www.forecasters.org): A nonprofit organization founded in 1982, it is dedicated to developing and furthering the generation, distribution and use of knowledge on forecasting. Its certificate program aims at facilitating improved forecasting practices in organizations. Topics that could be included in a certificate are (1) Introductory data collection and analysis; (2) Basic statistics; (3) Organization and management of forecasting; (4) Forecasting the economy and its impact on the firm; (5) Introductory econometrics.
- Association of Professional Futurists (www.apf.org): Founded in 2002 by an informal network of professional futurists, this global community promotes professional excellence, demonstrating the value of futures thinking. Futurists work in global corporations, small businesses, consultancies, education, nonprofits and governments. Its main purpose is to provide career opportunity for an analyst, speaker, manager or consultant to learn how to join its credentialed members to help stakeholders anticipate and influence the future. Its Career Center matches up professional futurists with marketplace opportunities, whether part-time as subcontractors or with full-time employment.
- Future Today Institute (https://futuretodayinstitute.com): Founded in 2006, the Future Today Institute researches, models and prototypes future risk and opportunity. As futurology management consultants to executive leadership teams worldwide, FTI's data-driven applied research reveals trends and calculates how they will disrupt business, government and society. The institute works with 75–80 organizations on their futures. The clients include Fortune 100 companies, government agencies, military communities, large organizations and investors both in the United States and abroad. It also offers Strategic Foresight Master Classes designed to teach teams methodology and tech/science trends in research.
- Futurist Institute (www.futuristinstitute.org): Founded in 2016, the institute provides the content and context for analysts to take longer-term views on business opportunities, risk management, markets and the economy for those interested in the future. The institute offers six tracks for certificates: Consulting, Legal, Accounting and tax, Financial planning, Standard professional and National security.

- Institute for Global Futures (https://globalfuturist.com): Founded by Dr. James Canton, the institute provides keynote presentations, strategy consulting and research services about future trends that will shape business, markets and society. Most of the institute's business is with the Global Fortune 1,000. The institute analyzes trends in many industries, such as health care, pharmaceuticals, retail, manufacturing, financial services, logistics, IT, media and others.

Senior Market Segments

The senior care market segment consists of three entities: product, service and application. Senior care *products* are specialized into housing, assistive devices and personal care products. Thanks to the rising demand for assistive devices in nursing and assisted living homes of senior patients, high-tech mobility devices such as walking canes, stairlifts, power wheelchairs, voice-activated lights and thermostats, and scooters are expected to dominate the growth of the senior care market in the forecast period of 2020 to 2027 (Data Bridge Market Research, 2020).

The senior care *service* market includes home care and adult day care. Aging-in-place services help seniors live safely at home as professional caregivers visit a senior's home to assist with daily living tasks. In a similar vein, adult day care aims to offer therapeutic exercise, mental interaction for participants, social activities appropriate for their condition and help with personal care such as grooming and using the toilet (AARP, 2019).

In terms of *application*, the senior care market will address the increase in the number of cardiovascular diseases such as arthritis, cataracts and heart diseases as well as neurological diseases such as Parkinson's and Alzheimer's. As age-related diseases evolve into the leading causes of death and health care costs in most advanced nations, anti-aging biotechnologies developed by pharmaceutical companies and Silicon Valley-based health care startups is expected to fuel the growth of senior care market (De Magalhães, Stevens & Thornton, 2017).

The senior economic market segment rests on the fact that the current generation of seniors, a significant consumer group in the digital age, has a large amount of disposable income; with a desire for guidance to live longer, healthier lives, they tend to be open minded to properly delivered marketing messages (Coray, 2018). Wolfgang Fengler of the Brookings Institution (2021) predicted that seniors would remain the wealthiest age group, as 76% of them worldwide will be active consumers through 2030, spending multiple trillions of dollars. Senior citizens tend to have both higher incomes than younger cohorts and higher needs for medical and specialized care (Fengler, 2021).

Similar to the senior care market, the senior economic market can be divided into three segments with different economic and financial spending power: underfunded yet still working, actively retiring and fully retired (Mule, 2015). The *still-working* segment encompasses a group of seniors who need to consider working longer than anticipated due to the lack of retirement income to maintain a preretirement standard of living. The *actively retiring* segment embraces those who are about to retire and plan to spend money during longer retirement years. The *fully retired* segment includes seniors who earn no active income but are affluent enough to spend a large amount of money from some combination of "savings, assets, pensions, Social Security, annuities and any other similar sources" (Mule, 2015, para. 17).

In the United States as well as worldwide, senior citizens controlled around 70% of disposable income in 2020. In the United States, senior citizens spent about 50% of all purchasing dollars, or five times the amount of the average American (Coray, 2018). U.S. seniors, by 2023, will account for 70% of disposable-income purchases. Such statistics on senior citizens are important to organizations, especially for corporations.

Impact: Strategic Communication for Organizations

Experts on integrated marketing communication, including advertising and public relations, advise organizations to look further into the senior citizen segment. For the next decade, inheritance money and spending of disposable income that current seniors have amassed will have a great influence on a wide range of industries and society as a whole. Dubbed "the great wealth transfer," U.S. seniors' leaving of an expected $30 trillion to their children and grandchildren will have major economic impacts. Moreover, spending for themselves will account for nearly $230 billion in sales of consumer-packaged goods and almost $90 billion a year spent on cars (Geller, 2019; Hall, 2019).

Despite the fact that an army of marketing experts enumerated a list of current and future market beneficiaries such as nursing homes, fancy resorts, luxury cars and anti-aging drugs in the senior citizen segment, scholars argue that applying seniors' personality and psychological traits (based on the most current social climate) to the prediction of their "temporal perspective" is key to marketing success in the senior market segment (Eastman, Modi & Gordon-Wilson, 2019; Navarro-Prados et al., 2018; Otoo et al., 2021).

The concept of temporal perspective describes how various aspects of time—past, present, and future—affect consumers' "motivation, cognition, and emotion, and therefore how they behave in relation to their specific goals"

(Wilson & Modi 2015, p. 3). Eastman, Modi and Gordon-Wilson (2019) summarized a present-time perspective as the indicator toward "immediate outcomes with consumers living for today and having little consideration for tomorrow" and a future-time perspective (FTP) as instructions for consumers "to strive for future goals and rewards" to be beneficial for future life outcomes (p. 279). After studying a sample of 520 American seniors representing a lucrative market segment, Eastman et al. (2019) found a significant positive relationship between FTP and conscientiousness on senior consumers' behavior. The findings demonstrated that seniors' personality can influence how they see time and how they adjust their disposable income to their purchasing behavior. In practice, corporations and brand marketers can learn how to communicate marketing messages to this rich consumer group based on their traits and time perspective, targeting seniors with beneficial compromises (agreeableness) and valuable products (conscientiousness) by ensuring an active and positive future (openness).

Otoo et al. (2021) extended previous senior traits-related consumer psychographic research to American and Chinese seniors' personality traits and identified how they affect motivation, preferences, sociodemographic and travel-related characteristics. They concluded that seniors' personality traits played a major role in making a purchasing or consumption decision; especially in the case of travel decisions, motivation served as a precursor to travel, meaning that senior citizens themselves debunked the old myth about their being close-minded and introverted. Instead, they actively seek new experiences and productive activities, including volunteering; the pursuit of successful aging leads them to search for and buy all kinds of goods and services other than the stereotypical reverse mortgages, erectile dysfunction pills and walk-in bathtubs (Baek et al., 2016).

Major brand marketers over the years were obsessed with a "segmented target audience by age"—18 to 34, 35 to 50, and over-55—since they used time-worn stereotypes about older people as needy and helpless (Beer, 2019). More recently, marketers and advertisers are likely to see the millennial and Gen. Z generations as the most exciting groups to promote their products to because they are market trend setters (Solomon, 2020), despite the fact that most of their disposable income is limited to the purchase of basic necessities and their spending habits are not yet fully established. More research outcomes demonstrate that the longtime paradigm of age segmentations in marketing needs to be reassessed and replaced. For example, a global 2017 study "Truth about Age" conducted by McCann Worldgroup, a leading global marketing services company, recommended marketers throw out the "age by the numbers" playbook. It instead suggested that the marketers shift from age to five attitudinal segmentations (2017, p. 10):

- The Ageless Adventurer: Sees aging as a journey of limitless opportunities and personal growth.
- The Communal Caretaker: Sees aging as a time of engaging with community and enriching personal relationships.
- The Actualizing Adult: Sees aging as a process of maturity and acquisition of adult responsibilities.
- The Future Fearer: Sees aging as a time of anxiety and uncertainty due to risks associated with old age.
- The Youth Chaser: Sees aging as a decline and loss of their youth and vitality.

One interesting finding from the study is that two-thirds of people over the age of 70 believe "you're never too old to casually date" and feel positive about the process of aging (2017, p. 5). Aging, according to the study, is an important facet of life that every generation thinks about; people in their 20s fear death the most, those in their 30s think about aging the most, while people in their 70s worry least about aging (p. 4). The study called on marketers to set a new paradigm regarding an approach to age across the age-driven marketing spectrum. In addition, four principles to guide marketers were proposed in terms of replacing the age segments with attitudinal segmentation:

1. Start Young: Aging is more a problem for the young generation. People in their 20s and 30s have a far more negative attitude toward getting older than older people do. Smart brands will find ways of beginning and reframing the age conversation much earlier (p. 8).
2. Celebrate the Gains: Too often the broader cultural conversation focuses on the "losses" associated with age, since aging was primarily framed as a negative process. There is an opportunity for brands to rewrite the narrative and focus on the gains at every age (p. 9)
3. Go Beyond the Number: Age in general has become a less useful predictor of behavior. Brands need to interrogate their own consumer segmentations in new ways to ensure that they are consistently going beyond the "number" (p. 10)
4. Promote Intergenerational Connections: There is one consistent theme that transcends markets when it comes to aging well: spending time with people of different younger and older ages. Intergenerational connections are seen as the key to aging well, but these are increasingly hard to come by in the modern marketing world (p. 11).

Nadia Tuma, senior vice president and director of McCann Worldgroup, who supervised the 2017 study, concluded that senior citizens want corporations and brands (1) to provide content that is educational, informative and more than just entertainment and (2) to envision an aging utopia where intergenerational connections are active (Beer, 2019).

Global Lessons for U.S. Strategic Communicators

The world is getting old. Many of the most advanced countries are expected to be categorized as super-aged countries by 2030, where more than one in five people (20%) are aged 65 or older. Japan, Finland, Portugal, Greece, Italy and Germany are already super-aged (see Box 9.2), and the United States, United Kingdom and Singapore will all be super-aged before 2050 (Gerontological Society of America, 2018).

By 2050, the total number of U.S. adults ages 65 and older is projected to rise to an estimated 85.7 million—roughly 20% of the overall population (Shalal, 2021; United Health Foundation, 2021). According to the United Nations, there were 703 million persons aged 65 years or over in the world in 2019. The number of older people is projected to double to 1.5 billion in 2050.

The world's population was projected to be 7.8 billion people on New Year's Day 2022. In raw numbers, 12% of China's population (see Box 9.3) is older than 65 (167 million seniors), followed by India (85 million) and the United States (54 million), according to Population Reference Bureau (2021). Asia and Europe are home to some of the world's oldest populations over 65—at the top, by share of the population, is Japan at 28%, followed by Italy, Finland, Portugal and Greece (United Nations, 2019).

Box 9.2. The World's Top 10 Super-Aged Societies (more than 20% 65 and older)

1. Japan
2. Italy
3. Portugal
4. Finland
5. Greece
6. Germany
7. Bulgaria
8. Malta
9. Croatia
10. France

Source: World Bank. (n.d.a).

Box 9.3. China's Aged Future

China's trend of a rapidly aging population is expected to accelerate in the coming decades, which will lead to overwhelming challenges for the Chinese economic and pension systems. Its fertility rate has failed to rise to at least 2.1, the minimum to maintain the existing size of the population (Paszak, 2020).

China's working-age population, aged 15 to 64, grew by at least 100 million people from 1990 to 2010, but the global financial crisis of 2009 influenced the nation's young people's thinking about having children (Buckley, 2015). The Chinese government, when ending the one-child policy, did not give much thought to the serious economic situation facing young couples.

In response to the low birthrate crisis, China announced in May 2021 that it would allow couples to have up to three children. The new policy was formally passed into law in August 2021, along with several resolutions aimed at boosting the birth rate and reducing the burden of raising a child (BBC News, 2021b).

Whereas Ling et al. (2021) suggested that the Chinese economy could be improved in the short term by delaying retirement age as a means of dealing with population aging, Cai and Du (2015) argued for constructing three pillars of its social protection system—the pension system, the medical care system and social assistance.

If the three-child policy does not increase the birth rate, China will continue to age. Such challenges in aging China pressure its government to deal with (1) senior citizens who show poor adaptability to technology, (2) industries offering mediocre quality of services toward senior citizens, (3) social norms of one-size-fits-all and the concept of the useless elderly and (4) shortage of qualified medical staff (Hu et al., 2021).

Although a majority of nations around world are expected to have at least 20% of their population aged 65 and over by 2050, experts on the economy and society are concerned about the rapid pace of aging in China (Cai & Du, 2015; Feng et al., 2018; Ling et al., 2021; O'Meara, 2020) and Germany (Kramer & Schreyogg, 2019; Schlomann et al., 2021; Schon & Stahler, 2020) due to both nations' global economic influences. The United States needs to learn from such aging nations to prepare for its own daunting challenges. In particular, many big-name U.S. brands and global corporations can plan ahead for their marketing and strategic communication strategies by learning lessons from other gray societies.

Germany

Germany, one of the "super-aged" societies with Japan, Finland, Italy and Greece, has a 65+ population that exceeds 21% of the total population (the

United States was 16.5% in 2019). A 2014 study, which found that 100 employed Germans supported about 40 senior citizens, predicted that by 2030 the ratio would rise to 85 elderly people per 100 German workers (Börsch-Supan, 2014). In addition, Germany's senior population over age 65 is projected to grow by 41% to 24 million by 2050, accounting for nearly one-third of the total population (FP Analytics, 2019). Germany, Europe's largest economy, will lose 5 million workers by the end of 2030 because of a demographic cliff, raising pressure on the national pension system, pushing higher inflation and skewing its intergenerational distribution (Kantchev, 2021). Economists and gerontologists forecast that Germans will face a frightening future of high prices on commodities, labor shortages and even higher taxes, while experiencing a heavy burden on family support by the millennial and Gen. Z generation when senior citizens become frail and unable to live independently (Börsch-Supan, 2014; Kramer & Schreyogg, 2019; Schon & Stahler, 2020).

The impact of population aging will take a heavy toll on the nation's economy. Schon and Stahler (2020) pointed out that when households become aware of this social phenomenon, with more older people and fewer younger people, they tend to increase their savings and reduce consumption in an attempt to prepare for their increased life expectancy, which results in their spending less and less over an extended retirement time span. As the German population ages, "the increase in capital per capita is smaller than the rise in capital intensity," meaning that "a relatively lower increase in capital per capita combined with a reduction in working-age population growth" will reduce the possibility to invest higher German savings domestically; thus per-capita consumption in the economy will fall (pp. 325–326). Such a regressive cycle of financial and economic activities deeply and passively affects the social security systems and the accumulation of aggregate wealth. As in the Chinese case, young Germans also struggle financially to marry and have a family during tough economic times.

Germany's birth rate in 2015 had already slumped to the lowest in the world (an average of 8.2 children were born per 1,000 inhabitants), even below Japan (8.4 children per 1,000 inhabitants), prompting concern about labor market shortages that would force employers to pay higher wages, which damages the economy in the long run (BBC News, 2015). The German government, in an effort to alleviate the pressure on economic growth and public finances due to its aging population, can implement retirement reforms—"raising the pensionable age and introducing flexible retirement options"—since Germany's Baby Boom generation began to reach the retirement age of 65 in 2019 (FP Analytics, 2019, pp. 15–20). Although retirement reforms serve as one possible solution to the economic problems of aging, other experts recommend a more practical approach to economic policy options: (1) accepting more young immigrant workers to fill the significant skills gap, establishing programs to provide "employment opportunities, education, and training" and (2) establishing a more labor-friendly policy for women, including childcare support (Cebulla & Wilkinson, 2019; Kostev, 2020; Schlomann et al., 2021).

It is interesting to note that both China and Germany, highly aware of their populations' aging, have taken different approaches. The Communist country focuses its policies and energy on increasing birthrates, while Europe's largest economy aims to increase labor force participation among older adults, immigrants and women, as well as retirement system reforms. Both countries are witnessing the rapid growth of senior market segment, especially for health care and wellness.

The German government aims to help senior citizens live independently through technology training and the development of specific technologies intended for seniors' use in the hopes that German senior citizens' level of digital competence will increase at a steady pace, evoking well-being and autonomy (Sommer, 2020). The German government's focus on raising seniors' level of digital competence, which can teach the U.S. government and marketers how to prepare for its upcoming super-aged society before 2030, includes the following elements:

- Establishment of a senior digital education programs: the government offers digital competency courses designed for senior citizens nationwide.
- Development of digital marketing tailored for senior citizens: brands and corporations would invest more resources in developing senior-friendly digital media content, even including web-savvy seniors called granfluencers, such as Helen Ruth Elam Van Winkle, 93, better known as Baddiewinkle, on Instagram with 3.4 million followers as of January 2022 (see Instagram @ baddiewinkle).

Digital Competence: Marketing of the Future

Ilomäki et al. (2014), who argued that the term *digital competence* could be understood as a synonym for digital literacy, defined the concept as "the ability to properly use and evaluate digital resources, tools and services, and apply it to lifelong learning processes" (Falloon, 2020, p. 2262).

Some 20 years ago, according to grandchildren's reports on 135 grandparents in the United States, seniors did lag seriously behind their grandchildren in technological comfort (Cooper-Chen, 2004). However, seniors in three Asian countries and Hong Kong were even farther behind their grandchildren, given that a quarter of U.S. grandparents used the internet, but only 1 of 473 Asian grandparents did.

Regarding current competence, American senior citizens' use of digital resources has significantly risen during COVID-19, which served as the bridge to close the generational tech divide, as seniors were encouraged to adopt technology in 2020 (Kakulla, 2021). From the early period of the coronavirus lockdown in 2020, people over 65 who faced loneliness and prolonged isolation motivated themselves to expand their tech literacy as a new survival skill. In other words, the coronavirus crisis gave them no choice but to learn and expand their use of technology devices for the first time, even including tablets, Amazon's Echo and smartwatches (AARP, 2021b). With such advanced tech devices, senior citizens use video chats (45%), texting (37%) and emailing (26%) more than before the pandemic, while streaming movies and TV shows and navigating the vast sea of online resources—beyond just Zoom (AARP, 2021b; Poon & Holder, 2020).

According to a 2017 study by Pew Research, 67% of American seniors used the internet and 42% owned smartphones. Without a doubt, from early 2020 both numbers have climbed or even soared after the U.S. coronavirus-driven lockdowns. Senior citizens moved parts of their social and work life online to combat loneliness and connect with their family and friends. Under new-normal lockdowns, they used video chats, ordered groceries online and embraced texting, email, social media posting, online shopping and content sharing.

However, not all seniors are adept at new tech because of knowledge gaps or because they lack the resources to purchase high-cost devices. More than half (54%) said they want a better grasp of the devices, with one in three feeling incompetent in the use of new technology (Kakulla, 2021). Ideally, government, nonprofits and corporations should focus on addressing these barriers by offering tech literacy classes and affordable tech devices. According to a survey conducted by a tech company (Poon & Holder, 2020), senior citizens during the COVID lockdowns hoped to

- receive tutorials on Zoom
- play gaming programs
- use telemedicine apps
- try ride-sharing apps
- participate in online dating
- exercise via virtual fitness classes

The survey clearly shows what U.S. brands and marketers can and should do for the present and future of the senior segment: offering (1) tech training, (2) affordable tech devices, (3) inspiring stories, (4) intergenerational connections and (5) simple, convenient, easy digital options. In sum, marketers should not fall prey to the myth that senior citizens in the United States lack tech knowledge and the desire to live actively in the digital age; rather, U.S. senior citizens tend to be active on email communication, smartphone texting, Facebook and the coronavirus-inspired use of Zoom.

Finally, marketers in the future should not ignore this current reality: 11% of TikTok users are 50 and older (Baig, 2021). TikTok, the most popular social app in the world—it overtook Facebook in 2020—is known as "the mood elevator" for all users of all ages (Manfred, 2021). The app will defy age boundaries as its demographics trend upward, especially among female seniors who have already started using TikTok videos as a delightful, uplifting "meditation vacation" to combat the depressing, anxiety-ridden pandemic reality (Im, 2021). More seniors will join and get active on TikTok over time, changing its milieu, although Gen. Z, millennials and Gen. X currently dominate the popular social media app. TikTok appeals to seniors' yearning for intergenerational connections, as the Four Gays can attest (see chapter 8).

As the wealthiest but most-ignored age group by U.S. marketers and advertisers, seniors receive only 5–10% of budgets (Geller, 2019). Senior citizens will appreciate more ads and marketing promotions customized for them through popular social media platforms. All brands, corporations and marketers ignore at their peril senior citizens' growing status as tech-savvy consumers with enviable disposable income.

Chapter 9. Projects and Exercises

1. Interview two or more 10-year-olds; after telling them they may live to age 104, ask them what they think the world will be like 100 years from now.
2. Interview someone who sells or designs aging-in-place products (e.g., stair lifts, voice-activated devices). How do they see future demand? How are they preparing for future customers? What marketing do they do?
3. Contact someone at one of the futures organizations (Box 9.1) for an open-ended discussion of the world as they see it 50 years from your own current age.
4. Talk to a number of seniors aged 65 and above. After your one-on-one discussions, using the McCann Worldgroups attitude segmentation guide outlined in this chapter, locate the seniors on the five-group spectrum.
5. Interview young-old seniors (in their 60s and 70s) and old-old seniors (in their 80s and 90s). How often do they use Zoom, Amazon (ordering items), texting and streaming services? How do the two groups compare?

Appendix A

SAMPLE PRESS RELEASE FROM LEADINGAGE

Template PRESS RELEASE for Communities/Organizations Who Are TESTING FOR COVID-19
Please Tailor as Needed and Distribute on Community/Organization Letterhead

FOR IMMEDIATE RELEASE
CONTACT: [INSERT NAME AND PHONE NUMBER]
A Statement from [INSERT COMMUNITY/ORGANIZATION NAME]

[insert day, month, year] [insert location]—A [resident/client/staff member] has been tested for COVID-19 of [insert organization].

On [Insert date], a [resident/client/staff member NO NAME.] reported precisely these symptoms, and the individual is presently being tested for COVID-19. As a preventive measure, we have already asked this individual to self-quarantine at home, and we are working closely with the [local Department of Health] to track and results and identify any other people with whom this [resident/client/staff member NO NAME] may have had close contact.

While we strive for transparency in everything we do, please know that we are bound by federal guidelines under the Health Insurance Portability and Accountability Act (HIPAA), which protects the privacy of our residents, who may not want their condition known. Our medical director follows all established federal laws in notifying families of any change in the medical condition of their loved ones. Our residents are our first priority.

If this [resident/client/staff member NO NAME] is confirmed to have a case of COVID-19, we will follow all CDC and [local Department of Health] instructions for additional testing, localized quarantine of other community members, and a thorough sanitation of all public areas.

Thank you, to all our community members, for your dedication, hard work, and commitment, today and every day. Together, we can ensure that [insert your community/organization name] has the best chance to stay ahead of the coronavirus.

We thank you for your cooperation and compliance with basic preventative measures we can all practice, such as good hand hygiene, social distancing and staying home when sick. Together, we can help everyone we care for stay healthy and well.

If you have questions or concerns, please reach out to [insert name] at [insert phone number] or [insert email address].

Used by permission from www.Leadingage.org

Appendix B
MEDIA PORTRAYALS

Age on the Small Screen: TV Comedies— Streaming

After Life, Netflix (Ricky Gervais). Tony's dad, who suffers from dementia, lives in an English care home that Tony visits every day. His dad dies in Season 2 of this comedy/drama.

The Kominsky Method, Netflix (Michael Douglas, Alan Arkin). Two aging show biz buddies navigate love and work in Los Angeles, a city that worships youth and beauty.

Grace and Frankie, Netflix (Jane Fonda, Lily Tomlin). In this comedy that explores gender roles and older-age sexuality, two husbands get divorced and remarried—to each other.

Golden Girls NBC, Hulu (Betty White). This 1985–1992 comedy depicts the lives of four mature women who live together in Miami. Betty White, who died December 31, 2021, aged 99, was the last surviving Golden Girl.

Age on the Silver Screen: 50 Years of Acclaimed English-Language Films

Harry and Tonto (1974). Art Carney won a Best Actor Oscar for a grumpy old man who makes a cross-country trip.

On Golden Pond (1981). Norman (Henry Fonda) and Ethel (Katherine Hepburn), long married, have a cottage, which their daughter (Jane Fonda) visits to try to repair her strained relationship with her father.

Cocoon (1985). The swimming pool of a Florida rental home has magical powers in this sci-fi film, for which Don Ameche won a Best Supporting Actor Oscar. Jessica Tandy, Hume Cronyn also star.

Driving Miss Daisy (1989). In the 1950s, the son (Dan Ackroyd) of an elderly Jewish widow (Jessica Tandy) hires a Black driver (Morgan Freeman), who eventually wins over Miss Daisy as a friend, not a servant.

Grumpy Old Men (1993). Jack Lemon and Walter Matthau play feuding neighbors who go ice fishing and play pranks on each other. Then Ann-Margaret enters the picture, upsetting the dynamic of the neighborhood.

The Straight Story (1999). Richard Farnsworth, handicapped in real life, goes to visit his brother in a riding mower. David Lynch directed.

Iris (2001). Judi Dench, nominated for a Best Actress Oscar, played Iris Murdoch in this biographical depiction of the free-spirited English philosopher and novelist, who lived 1919–1999.

Something's Got to Give (2003). Jack Nicholson plays a bachelor, 63, who dates women in their 30s; Diane Keaton plays an author in her 50s, who goes out with a young doctor. Eventually the two elders "find" each other.

Away from Her (2006). Julie Christie, who must go into a nursing home because of her severe Alzheimer's, eventually does not recognize her husband and starts a relationship with another man at the facility.

The Curious Case of Benjamin Button (2008). Brad Pitt plays a character (loosely based on one created by F. Scott Fitzgerald) who ages backward. He hopes to intersect with his true love (Cate Blanchett) at the right age for both.

The Iron Lady (2011). Meryl Streep, who won an Oscar and Golden Globe for this role, plays Margaret Thatcher looking back on her life as she develops dementia, with past and present merging.

The Best Exotic Marigold Hotel (2011). Judi Dench and Maggie Smith play British retirees who decide to retire to a luxurious and reasonably priced hotel in India, which turns out to be less than as advertised.

Quartet (2012). Maggie Smith, a Golden Globe nominee for Best Actress, plays a former opera star who moves into a home for retired musicians, where a former beau happens to also live. Gorgeous score.

Grandma (2015). Lily Tomlin stars as a lesbian poet whose granddaughter (Julia Garner) asks for money to pay for an abortion. Tomlin was nominated for a Golden Globe for her role in this low-budget film.

Going in Style (2017). In this heist comedy, three disgruntled friends (Morgan Freeman, Michael Caine, Alan Arkin) aim to get back at the bank that took away their pensions.

Good Luck to You, Leo Grande (2022). A 63-year-old widow (Emma Thompson), who had an unsatisfying sexual relation with her husband for 31 years, hires sex worker Leo Grande to try to experience what she has missed.

Appendix C
RESOURCES FOR RESEARCH

Alzheimer's Association
www.Alzheimer's.org
800-272-3900
225 N. Michigan Ave., floor 17, Chicago, IL 60601
Established in 1980, it is "the leading voluntary health organization in Alzheimer's care, support and research." A 501(c)(3) charity, it has 81 local chapters—54 traditional plus 27 affiliates. Purple is its official color. June is Alzheimer's and Brain Awareness Month; November is Alzheimer's Awareness Month; September 21 is World Alzheimer's Day. It publishes a magazine, *ALZ*, four times a year.

AARP
aarp.org
888-687-2277
601 East St. NW
Washington, DC 20049
Established in 1958 by Ethel Percy Andrus in Ojai, CA, it claims 38 million members. Focus is persons 50 and older. Originally called the American Association of Retired Persons, it changed its name to the four letters AARP in 1999. It has 2,250 staff members. In 2019, its expenses were $1.696 billion. It is a 501(c)(4) (a social welfare group, donations to which are not tax deductible). Publishes *AARP The Magazine* and *AARP Bulletin*.

Death with Dignity
deathwithdignity.org
The organization has its web server in Canada. It reports that 16 states introduced bills in 2022 legislative sessions, but as of this writing, only Massachusetts

has a pending bill that may succeed. Currently, the District of Columbia and these states have statutes: Colorado, Hawaii, Maine, New Jersey, New Mexico, Oregon and Washington. California and Vermont have passed legislation that increases patient options.

Diverse Elders Coalition
diverse elders.org
646-653-5015
305 7th Ave., 15th floor
New York, NY 10001
Established in 2010, it encompasses five member organizations: the National Asian Pacific Center on Aging, the National Caucus and Center on Black Aging Inc., the National Hispanic Council on Aging, SAGE, and Southeast Asia Resource Action Center. See separate entries. Lauren Pognan serves as national director.

LeadingAge
www.LeadingAge.org
202-783-2242
2519 Connecticut Ave. NW
Washington, DC 20008
Established in 1961 when a group of nonprofit organizations joined together to "inspire our country to view aging differently." In 2010, the members approved a name change to reflect a redefined identity. A 501(c)(3), it has more than 5,000 members and 38 state partners. Katie Smith Sloan serves as CEO, as well as being executive director of the Global Ageing Network, which has a presence in more than 50 countries.

National Asian Pacific Center on Aging
www.napca
206-624-1221
Melbourne Tower
1511 3rd Ave. #914
Seattle, WA 98101
Established in 1979, NAPCA helps Asian-American elders overcome cultural, linguistic and economic obstacles. Its website, which offers a choice of 29 languages, states, "We envision a society in which all Asian American and Pacific Islanders age with dignity and well-being."

National Association of Senior Move Managers
248-442-5859
P.O. Box 209
Hinsdale, IL 60522
"Recognizing and managing the stress of relocating older adults, individuals and families. . . . All members must meet strict vetting requirements."

National Caucus and Center on Black Aging
www.ncba-aging.org
202-637-8400
1220 L St. NW, suite 800
Washington, DC 20005
Established in 1970, the organization, a 501(c)(3), aims at "making minority participation in aging services a national issue and priority." Karyn Jones, who served eight years in the Texas House of Representative, leads the NCCBA. It calls itself "the oldest and most effective voice for African American and low-income minority services."

National Council on Aging
www.ncoa.org
571-527-3982
251 18th St. South, suite 500
Arlington, VA 22202
Established in 1950 as "the first national center for older adults." It aims to improve all older (age 55-plus) adults' lives, "especially women, people of color, LGBTQ+, low-income and rural individuals." NCOA, an advocacy organization, helps strengthen the 11,000 U.S. senior centers, partly by promoting September as National Senior Center Month. Simona Combi is the public relations manager.

National Hispanic Council on Aging
www.nhcoa.org
202-347-9733
2201 12th St. NW, Suite 101
Washington, DC 20009
Established in 1969, it was incorporated in Denver in 1980. Dr. Yantra Cruz serves as president and CEO. By 2060, the number of Hispanics aged 65 and over is expected to constitute 21% of the U.S. elderly population. One NHCOA priority involves getting Hispanics in clinical trials, above the current 8% of those enrolled in trials.

Milken Institute, Center for the Future of Aging
milkensintitute.org
202-336-8900
730 15th St. NW
Washington, DC 20005
"The center works to improve lives and build a better future for all ages." It advocates for "healthy longevity and financial wellness" through health summits, conferences and media activities worldwide. Nora Super is the executive director. Chad Clinton, is director, media relations.

Services and Advocacy for Gay Elders (SAGE)
www.sageusa.org
212-741-2247
305 7th Ave., 15th floor
New York, NY 10001
Established in 1978 by Doug Kimmel, cofounder. SAGE has 30 affiliates in 21 states and Puerto Rico. It advocates for nondiscrimination in housing and other issues affecting older LGBTQ adults.

USC Center for Elder Justice
USC Leonard Davis School of Gerontology
University of Southern California
3620 So. Vermont Ave.
Los Angeles, CA 90089
eldermistreatment.usc.edu
Founded by Judith Tamkin, the Center for Elder Justice aims to prevent financial exploitation, physical abuse and neglect. Various departments of the University of Southern California cooperate on research and solutions on mistreatment of older citizens.

Works Cited

AARP. (n.d.a). About AARP. https://www.aarp.org/membership

AARP. (n.d.b). Tap into a powerful audience with AARP media. https://advertise.aarp.org

AARP. (2019, Oct. 3). Adult day care: What family caregivers need to know. https://www.aarp.org/caregiving/home-care/info-2017/adult-day-care.html

AARP. (2020, Oct. 23). 95 percent of Americans killed by COVID-19 were 50 or over. https://www.aarp.org/health/conditions-treatments/info-2020/coronavirus-deaths-older-adults.html

AARP. (2021a). AARP's chief communications and marketing officer delivers a clear and consistent mission. https://www.aarp.org/about-aarp/info-2021/martha-boudreau-interview.html

AARP. (2021b, April 21). Tech usage among older adults skyrockets during pandemic. Press release. https://press.aarp.org/2021-4-21-Tech-Usage-Among-Older-Adults-Skyrockets-During-Pandemic

AARP The Magazine. (n.d.). 2021 media kit. https://res.cloudinary.com/advertise-aarp/image/upload/v1611250158/ATM_2021_Media_Kit_1.21.21.pdf

Adams, R. (2019, Dec. 31). All robot dogs go to the cloud. *Buzzfeed News*. https://www.buzzfeednews.com/article/rosalindadams/aibo-robot-dogs-japan

Adams, R. G. (1997). Friendship patterns among older women. In J. M. Coyle (Ed.), *Handbook on women and aging* (pp. 400–417). Greenwood.

Aizawa, K. (2014, May 19). Paid retirement homes, where to choose. *President Online*. https://president.jp/articles/-/17125?pages=4

Aldoory, L., & Toth, E. (2021). *The future of feminism in public relations and strategic communication*. Rowman & Littlefield.

American Marketing Association (AMA). (n.d.). https://www.ama.org/the-definition-of-marketing-what-is-marketing

Annuity.org. (n.d.). 50+ Essential retirement statistics for 2022. https://www.annuity.org/retirement/retirement-statistics

Applegate, W., & Ouslander, J. (2020). COVID-19 presents high risk to older persons. *Journal of the American Geriatric Society, 68*(4), 681.

Appold, K. (2017, Feb. 10). Effective communication among different generations. *The Rheumatologist.* https://www.the-rheumatologist.org/article/effective-communication-among-different-generations

Appold, S. J., Johnson, J. H., & Parnell, A. M. (2015). Market needs and economic impact of continuing care retirement communities in North Carolina. Frank Hawkins Kenan Institute of Private Enterprise, University of North Carolina–Chapel Hill. https://www.kenaninstitute.unc.edu/wp-content/uploads/2017/09/2015_CCRC_Economic_Impact_St.pdf

Arber, S., & Ginn, J. (1991). *Gender and later life. A sociological analysis of resources and constraints.* Sage.

Argentum. (2020). 2020 largest provider list: A closer look at the 150 largest providers in senior living, plus a post-COVID-19 outlook. https://www.argentum.org/wp-content/uploads/2020/08/2020-Largest-Provider-Report_Final.pdf

Arias, E., Tejada-Vera, B., & Ahmad, F. (2021). Provisional life expectancy estimates for January through June, 2020. CDC. https://www.cdc.gov/nchs/data/vsrr/VSRR10-508.pdf

Ariella, S. (2021, May 21). 10 largest nursing home companies in the United States. ZIPPIA. https://www.zippia.com/advice/largest-nursing-home-companies

Auestad, R. A. (2009). Long-term care insurance, marketization and the quality of care: "Good time living" in a recently established nursing home in a suburb of Tokyo. *Japan Forum, 21*(2), 209–231. Doi: 10.1080/09555801003679124

Auxier, B., & Anderson, M. (2021, April 7). Social media use in 2021. Pew Research Center. https://www.pewresearch.org/internet/2021/04/07/social-media-use-in-2021

Avery, E. J., Lariscy, R. W., Kim, S., & Hocke, T. (2010). A quantitative review of crisis communication research in public relations from 1991 to 2009. *Public Relations Review, 36,* 190–192.

Baek, Martin, P., Siegler, I. C., Davey, A., & Poon, L. W. (2016). Personality traits and successful aging: Findings from the Georgia Centenarian Study. *International Journal of Aging & Human Development, 83*(3), 207–227. https://doi.org/10.1177/0091415016652404

Bagozzi, R. P., Gopinath, M., & Nyer, P. U. (1999). The role of emotions in marketing. *Journal of the Academy of Marketing Science, 27,* 184–206. https://doi.org/10.1177/0092070399272005

Bagozzi, R., Belanche, D., Casaló, L. V., & Flavián, C. (2016). The role of anticipated emotions in purchase intentions. *Psychology & Marketing, 33*(8), 629–645. https://doi.org/10.1002/mar.20905

Baig, E. (2021, July 26). Surprise! TikTok app defies age boundaries. AARP Family. https://www.aarp.org/home-family/personal-technology/info-2021/tiktok-app-defies-age-boundaries.html

Baiocchi-Wagner, E. A. (2012). Framing the aging experience in care facility brochures: A mixed-method analysis. *Southern Communication Journal, 77*(4), 349–368.

Balazs, A. (1995). The use and image of mature adults in health care advertising (1954–1989). *Health Marketing Quarterly, 12*(3), 10–26.

Balis, J. (2021, March 10). Truths about marketing after the pandemic. *Harvard Business Review, 10.* https://hbr.org/2021/03/10-truths-about-marketing-after-the-pandemic

Bartel, O. (2015). *Postmodern advertising in Japan.* University Press of New England.

Bartikowski, B., Laroche, M., & Richard, M. (2019). A content analysis of fear appeal advertising in Canada, China and France. *Journal of Business Research, 103,* 232–239.

Batchelor, L. (2022, Jan. 21). Digital marketing trends in 2022: How to tap into them. The Drum. https://www.thedrum.com/opinion/2022/01/21/digital-marketing-trends -2022-how-tap-them

Baughman, J. (1998). The transformation of *Time* magazine: From opinion leader to supporting player. *Media Studies Journal, 12*(3), 120–127.

BBC News. (2015, May 29). Germany passes Japan to have world's lowest birth rate— study. https://www.bbc.com/news/world-europe-32929962

BBC World Service. (2021a, July 9). The pandemic brings more robots. The real story. https://www.bbc.co.uk/programmes/w3ct1hsm

BBC World Service. (2021b, Aug. 20). China NPC: Three-child policy formally passed into law. https://www.bbc.com/news/world-asia-china-58277473

Beer, J. (2019, May 6). Why marketing to seniors is so terrible. Fastcompany. https:// www.fastcompany.com/90341477/why-marketing-to-seniors-is-so-terrible

Benes, R. (2018, April 30). Improving audience segmentation is top campaign manage- ment goal. Emarketer.com. https://www.emarketer.com/content/improving-audience -segmentation-is-top-campaign-management-goal

Benesse Style Care. (2019). What is housing for the elderly? https://kaigo.benesse-style -care.co.jp/merit

Benoit, W. L. (1995). *Accounts, excuses, and apologies: A theory of image restoration strate- gies.* State University of New York Press.

Benoit, W. L. (1997). Image repair discourse and crisis communication. *Public Relations Review, 23,* 177–186.

Bernard, M., Phillips, J., Machin, L., & Davies, V. H. (Eds.). (2000). *Women ageing: Changing identities, challenging myths.* Routledge.

Berraies, K., Hannachi, M., & Yahia, K. B. (2017). Identifying the effects of perceived values of mobile banking applications on customers: Comparative study between baby boomers, generation X and generation Y. *International Journal of Bank Marketing, 35*(6), 1018–1038. https://doi.org/10.1108/IJBM-09-2016-013

Berry, S., & Barnett, T. (2019, May 7). The graveyard of old diseases. CSI: Dixie. Univer- sity of Georgia. https://csidixie.org/numbers/mortality-census/graveyard-old-diseases

Bilodeau, Kelly. (2022, Feb.1). FTC orders refunds to people who purchased anti- aging products. Harvard Health Publishing. https://www.health.harvard.edu/staying -healthy/ftc-orders-refunds-to-people-who-purchased-anti-aging-products.

Bookman, A. (2008) Innovative models of aging in place: Transforming our communi- ties for an aging population. *Community, Work & Family, 11*(4), 419–438.

Börsch-Supan, A. (2014). Aging population: Problems and policy options in the US and Germany. *Economic Policy, 6*(12), 103–140. https://doi.org/10.2307/1344450

Bradley, D., & Longino, C. Jr. (2001). How older people think about images of aging in advertising and the media. *Generations, 25*(3), 17–21.

Bramlett-Solomon, S., & Subramanian, G. (1999). Nowhere near perfect: Images of the elderly in *Life* and *Ebony* magazine ads, 1990–1997. *Journalism Quarterly, 76*(3), 565–572.

Bramlett-Solomon, S., & Wilson, V. (1989). Images of the elderly in *Life* and *Ebony*, 1978–1987. *Journalism Quarterly, 66*(1), 185–188.

Brasor, P., & Tsukuba, M. (2014, Jan. 6). Retirement homes come of age in booming market. *Japan Times*. https://www.japantimes.co.jp/community/2014/01/06/how-tos/retirement-homes-come-of-age-in-booming-market/#.Xo1GZMhKjIU

Breeding, B. (2018a, Dec. 10). New study shows CCRC residents ARE happier and healthier. MyLifeSite. https://mylifesite.net/blog/post/ccrc-residents-are-happier-and-healthier

Breeding, B. (2018b, Sep. 24). A closer look: Examining the CCRC market in the U.S. My Life Site. https://mylifesite.net/blog/post/examining-ccrc-market-in-u-s

Britannica. (n.d.). Silver. https://www.britannica.com/science/silver

Browning, M. (2021). The definitive *Golden Girls* cultural reference guide. Lyons Press/Rowman & Littlefield.

Brueggemann, T. (2021, Feb. 23). *Monster Hunter* and *Greenland* lead VOD charts, while '*Croods 2*' remains unstoppable. *IndieWire*. https://www.indiewire.com/2021/02/monster-hunter-greenland-lead-vod-charts-croods-2-1234618476

Buckley, C. (2015, Oct. 29). China ends one-child policy, allowing families two children. *The New York Times*. https://www.nytimes.com/2015/10/30/world/asia/china-end-one-child-policy.html

Burch, A. (2021, Aug. 12). The Villages, a retirement community in Florida, was the fastest-growing metro area over the last decade. *The New York Times*. https://www.nytimes.com/2021/08/12/us/the-villages-census-florida-population.html

Busch, A. (2019, Feb. 27). The invisibility of older women. *The Atlantic*. https://www.theatlantic.com/entertainment/archive/2019/02/akiko-busch-mrs-dalloway-shows-aging-has-benefits/583480

Butler, R. (1969). Ageism: Another form of bigotry. *The Gerontologist, 9*(3), 243–246.

Cai, F., & Du, Y. (2015). The social protection system in ageing China. *Asian Economic Policy Review, 10*(2), 250–270. https://doi.org/10.1111/aepr.12103

Calasanti, T., & Slevin, K. (2001). *Gender, social inequalities and aging*. AltaMira.

Cancel, A., Cameron, G., Sallot, L., & Mitrook, M. (1997). It depends: A contingency theory of accommodation in public relations. *Journal of Public Relations Research, 9*(1), 31–63.

Cancel, A., Mitrook, M., & Cameron, G. (1999). Testing the contingency theory of accommodation in public relations. *Public Relations Review, 25*(2), 171–197.

Candidsky. (2021, Oct. 1). Baby Boomers go digital: How the pandemic affected baby boomer's online behaviour. https://www.candidsky.com/blog/baby-boomers-go-digital-how-the-pandemic-affected-baby-boomers-online-behaviour

Carol Woods News. (2022, March). A service of remembrance, p. 6.

CDC. (n.d.). Nursing home care. https://www.cdc.gov/nchs/fastats/nursing-home-care.htm

CDC. (2019). Long-term care providers and services users in the United States, 2015–2016. Retrieved from https://www.cdc.gov/nchs/data/series/sr_03/sr03_43-508.pdf

CDC. (2020). COVID-19. https://covid.cdc.gov/covid-data-tracker/#datatracker-home

Cebulla, A., & Wilkinson, D. (2019). Responses to an ageing workforce: Germany, Spain, the United Kingdom. *Business Systems Research, 10*(1), 120–137. https://doi.org/10.2478/bsrj-2019-0009

Centers for Medicare and Medicaid Services. (n.d.a). Find and compare health care providers. https://www.medicare.gov/forms-help-resources/find-compare-health-care-providers

Centers for Medicare and Medicaid Services. (n.d.b). Medicare coverage of skilled nursing facility care. https://www.medicare.gov/Pubs/pdf/10153-Medicare-Skilled-Nursing-Facility-Care.pdf

Chambers, P. (2000). Widowhood in later life. In M. Bernard, J. Phillips, L. Machin, & V. H. Davies (Eds.), *Women aging: Changing identities, challenging myths* (pp. 127–147). Routledge.

Charles, S. T., & Carstensen, L. L. (2010). Social and emotional aging. *Annual Review of Psychology, 61,* 383–409. https://doi.org/10.1146/annurev.psych.093008.100448

Chen, Y., & Ma, X. (2009). Age differences in risky decisions: The role of anticipated emotions. *Educational Gerontology, 35,* 575–586. doi: 10.1080/03601270802605291

Cheng, H. (1997). Toward an understanding of cultural values manifest in advertising: A content analysis of Chinese television commercials in 1990 and 1995. *Journalism and Mass Communication Quarterly, 74*(4), 773–796.

Chidabaram, P. (2020, April 23). State reports of cases and deaths in long-term care facilities. Kaiser Family Foundation. https://www.kff.org/coronavirus-covid-19/issue-brief/state-reporting-of-cases-and-deaths-due-to-covid-19-in-long-term-care-facilities

Chidabaram, P., Garfield, R., & Neuman, T. (2020, Nov. 25). COVID-19 has claimed the lives of 100,000 long-term care residents and staff. Kaiser Family Foundation. https://www.kff.org/policy-watch/covid-19-has-claimed-the-lives-of-100000-long-term-care-residents-and-staff

Chies, P. (2022). *Pratt's long-term care: Managing across the continuum* (5th ed.). Jones & Bartlett Learning.

Chopik, W. J., Bremner, R. H., Johnson, D. J., & Giasson, H. L. (2018). Age differences in age perceptions and developmental transitions. *Frontiers in Psychology, 9,* 67. https://doi.org/10.3389/fpsyg.2018.00067

CHPA. (Oct. 2020). Too big to ignore: Boomers are an ideal market for the self-care products sector. CHPA Insights. https://www.chpa.org/sites/default/files/media/docs/2020-10/Too-Big-to-Ignore-10142020.pdf

Colapinto, J. (2021, Dec. 6). New retirement village attracts Jimmy Buffett fans. *AARP The Magazine,* pp. 46–50.

Coming of Age. (n.d.). 7 tips for effectively messaging to seniors. https://www.comingofage.com/blog/7-tips-for-effectively-messaging-to-seniors

Commission on Accreditation of Rehabilitation Facilities (CARF). (n.d.). About us. www.carf.org

Coombs, W. T. (1995). Choosing the right words: The development of guidelines for the selection of the "appropriate" crisis-response strategies. *Management Communication, 8,* 447–476.

Coombs, W. T. (2009). Conceptualizing crisis communication. In R. L. Health, & H. D. O'Hair (Eds.), *Handbook of risk and crisis communication* (pp. 99–118). Taylor & Francis.

Coombs, W. T., & Holladay, S. J. (1996). Communication and attribution in a crisis: An experimental study in crisis communication. *Journal of Public Relations Research, 8*(4), 279–295.

Cooper-Chen, A. (2004). Cyberlag: Over-65s' internet adoption and usage in Japan, South Korea, China, Taiwan and the United States. *Media Asia, 31*(4), 211–217.

Cooper-Chen, A., Leung, E., & Cho, Sung-ho. (1994). The image of women in East Asian magazine advertising, 1989–1990. Paper presented to the International Association for Mass Communication Research, Seoul.

Coray. (2018, Aug. 26). Why market to seniors? Shreerid. https://www.sheerid.com/blog/how-to-market-to-seniors

Costa, A. (June 1, 2021). 3 reasons why you should turn your social media attention to baby boomers. The Drum. https://www.thedrum.com/opinion/2021/06/01/3-reasons-why-you-should-turn-your-social-media-attention-baby-boomers

Covello, V. (2003). Best practices in public health risk and crisis communication. *Journal of Health Communication, 8,* 5–8. DOI: 10.1080/10810730390224802

Cronin, M. (2009, Mar 9). Slideshows in web designs, when and how to use them. *Smashing Magazine.* https://www.smashingmagazine.com/2009/03/slideshows-in-web-design-when-and-how-to-use-them

Data Bridge Market Research. (2020). Global elderly care market—industry trends and forecast to 2027. https://www.databridgemarketresearch.com/reports/global-elderly-care-market

Davis, P. (2017, Feb. 9). Did Super Bowl marketers score a touchdown with Boomers? Campaign US. https://www.campaignlive.com/article/super-bowl-marketers-score-touchdown-boomers/1423708

De Magalhães, J. P., Stevens, M., & Thornton, D. (2017). The business of anti-aging science. *Trends in Biotechnology (Regular Ed.), 35*(11), 1062–1073. https://doi.org/10.1016/j.tibtech.2017.07.004de

de Rugy, V., & Leventhal, J. (2018, April 26). How many workers pay the benefits of each social security retiree? Mercatus Center, George Mason University. https://www.mercatus.org/publications/social-security/how-many-workers-pay-benefits-each-social-security-retiree

DesRochers, M. (2021, March 4). How corporate communications can be most effective. Ragan. https://www.ragan.com/how-corporate-communications-can-be-most-effective

Dooley, B. (2019, Dec. 24). Japan shrinks by 500,000 people as births fall to lowest number since 1874. *The New York Times.* https://www.nytimes.com/2019/12/24/world/asia/japan-birthrate-shrink.html

Dudley, D. (2016, Nov.). A permanent vacation under the Florida sun. *AARP Bulletin.* https://www.aarp.org/work/retirement-planning/info-2016/the-good-life-in-florida.html

Duke University. (2020, March 24). Older people generally more emotionally healthy, better able to resist daily temptations. *ScienceDaily.* www.sciencedaily.com/releases/2020/03/200324202043.htm

Dychtwald, K. (2021, Sept.). Ageism: Alive and well in advertising. *AARP Bulletin,* 6–9.

Eastman, J., Modi, P., & Gordon-Wilson, S. (2019). The impact of future time perspective and personality on the sustainable behaviours of seniors. *Journal of Consumer Policy, 43*(2), 275–294. https://doi.org/10.1007/s10603-019-09440-1

Edwards, E. (2020, Oct. 26). The modern-day communicator's manifesto. Medium .com. https://elizabeth-edwards.medium.com/the-modern-day-communicators -manifesto-4ee699d813f6

Eser, Z., Isin, F. B., & Tolon, M. (2011). Perceptions of marketing academics, neurologists, and marketing professionals about neuromarketing. *Journal of Marketing Management, 27*(7–8), 854–868. https://doi.org/10.1080/02672571003719070

Esswein, P. M., & Block, S. (2014, July 31). Retire in style at a continuing care retirement community: Continuing care retirement communities offer a resort-like setting and care when you need it. *Kiplinger.* https://www.kiplinger.com/article/retirement/ t010-c000-s002-ccrc-continuing-care-retirement-community.html

Falloon, G. (2020). From digital literacy to digital competence: The teacher digital competency (TDC) framework. *Educational Technology Research and Development, 68*(5), 2449–2472. https://doi.org/10.1007/s11423-020-09767-4

Famakinwa, J. (2021, July 20). Aging-in-place market valued at $151b, but still overshadowed by other care settings. *Home Health Care News.* https://homehealthcare news.com/2021/07/aging-in-place-market-valued-at-151b-but-still-overshadowed-by -other-care-settings

Farley, R. (2020, July 24). Do pharmaceutical companies spend more on marketing than research and development? https://www.pharmacychecker.com/askpc/pharma -marketing-research-development/

Faverio, M. (2022, Jan. 13). Share of those 65 and older who are tech users has grown in the past decade. Pew Research Center. https://www.pewresearch.org/fact-tank/2022/ 01/13/share-of-those-65-and-older-who-are-tech-users-has-grown-in-the-past-decade

Fearn-Banks, K. (2016*). Crisis communications: A casebook approach* (5th ed.). Routledge.

Felsenthal, E. (2018, Oct. 1), A new era for TIME. *Time, 192*(13), 2.

Feng, Q., Yeung, W., Wang, Z., & Zeng, Y. (2018). Age of retirement and human capital in an aging China, 2015–2050. *European Journal of Population, 35*(1), 29–62. https://doi.org/10.1007/s10680-018-9467-3

Fengler, W. (Jan. 14, 2021). The silver economy is coming of age: A look at the growing spending power of seniors. The Brookings Institution. https://www.brookings.edu/ blog/future-development/2021/01/14/the-silver-economy-is-coming-of-age-a-look-at -the-growing-spending-power-of-seniors

Ferguson, S. (2015). Public relations planning. In W. Donsbach (Ed.), *The concise encyclopedia of communication* (pp. 507–509). Wiley.

Fingerman, K., Pillemer, K., Silverstein, M., & Suitor, J. (2021). The Baby Boomers' intergenerational relationships. *The Gerontologist, 52*(2), 199–209. https://doi.org/ 10.1093/geront/gnr139

FP Analytics. (2019). *The aging readiness and competitiveness report.* https://arc.aarpinter national.org/File%20Library/Full%20Reports/ARC-Report---Germany.pdf

Freedonia. (2018). Industry study 3214: Elder care services. https://www.freedoniagroup .com/industry-study/elder-care-services-3214.htm

Gaille, B. (2016, March 21). 43 distressing *Time* magazine demographics. Brandongaille. https://www.Brandongaille.com/43-distressing-time-magazine-demographics

Gantz, W., Gartenberg, H., & Rainbow, C. (1980). Approaching invisibility: The portrayal of the elderly in magazine advertisements. *Journal of Communication, 30*, 56–60.

Garber, M. (2018, March 20). Jagged little (blue) pill. *The Atlantic.* https://www.the-atlantic.com/entertainment/archive/2018/03/20-years-of-viagra/556343

Geller, G. (2019, Aug. 22). Baby Boomers spend more than millennials—yet are ignored by advertisers. *Media Post.* https://www.mediapost.com/publications/article/336177/baby-boomers-spend-more-than-millennials-yet-ar.html

Gerashi, K., & Fakhreddin, F. (2021). Influence of emotions on purchase loyalty among child consumers: The moderating role of family communication patterns. *Journal of Marketing Analytics, 9*(4), 298–310. https://doi.org/10.1057/s41270-020-00095-3

Gerontological Society of America. (2018). Longevity economics. https://www.geron.org/images/gsa/documents/gsa-longevity-economics-2018.pdf

Giffin, E. (2021). Marketing to Baby Boomers: Understanding the Boomer generation's buying habits. *Ecommerce News.* https://www.bigcommerce.com/blog/baby-boomer-marketing/#conclusion

Giles, E. (2020, Aug. 26). 10 Baby Boomer marketing strategies that drive leads. Bluleadz. https://www.bluleadz.com/blog/10-marketing-strategies-targeting-baby-boomers

Graham, J. (2021, Oct. 20). "They treat me like I'm old and stupid": Seniors decry health providers' age bias. *Kaiser Health News.* https://khn.org/news/article/ageism-health-care-seniors-decry-bias-inappropriate-treatment

Gramlich, J. (2022, March 3). Two years into the pandemic, Americans inch closer to a new normal. Pew Research Center. https://www.pewresearch.org/2022/03/03/two-years-into-the-pandemic-americans-inch-closer-to-a-new-normal

Green, S. (1991, Nov.). A two-faced society. *Nursing Times, 13,* 30–31.

Gregerson, J. (2020, June 9). What history tells us about vaccine timetables. Charles River Laboratories. https://www.criver.com/eureka/what-history-tells-us-about-vaccine-timetables

Groger, L., & Kinney, J. (2006). CCRC here we come! Reasons for moving to a continuing care retirement community. *Journal of Housing for the Elderly, 20*(4), 79–101.

Grunig, L. Toth, E., & Hon, L. (2000). Feminist values in public relations. *Journal of Public Relations Research, 12*(1), 49–68.

Guo, K. L., & Castillo, R. J. (2012). The U.S. long-term care system: Development and expansion of naturally occurring retirement communities as an innovative model for aging in place. *Ageing Int, 37,* 210–227. doi: 10.1007/s12126-010-9105-9

Ha, J. H., & Riffe, D. (2015). Crisis-related research in communication and business journals: An interdisciplinary review from 1992 to 2011. *Public Relations Review, 41,* 569–578.

Haas, A., McDougal, T., & Herrin, J. (2020, July 21). Seven considerations for building an effective messaging strategy. Deloitte Digital. https://www.deloittedigital.com/us/en/blog-list/2020/seven-considerations-for-building-an-effective-messaging-strateg.html

Hackley, C. (1999). An epistemological odyssey: Toward social construction of the advertising process. *Journal of Marketing Communication, 5,* 157–168.

Hall, M. (2019, Nov. 11). The greatest wealth transfer in history: What's happening and what are the implications. *Forbes.* https://www.forbes.com/sites/markhall/2019/11/11/the-greatest-wealth-transfer-in-history-whats-happening-and-what-are-the-implications/?sh=4975d6904090

Hamilton, M. (2021, Sept. 11). Does the supplement Prevagen improve memory? A court case is asking that question. *The Washington Post.* https://www.washingtonpost.com/health/prevagen-memory-loss-does-it-work/2021/09/10/53e5d3e8-f3a6-11eb-a49b-d96f2dac0942_story.html

Hangley, B. (2022, September). Your all-in-one retirement home? *AARP Bulletin,* p. 20.

Heath, R. L. (Ed.). (2013). *Encyclopedia of public relations* (2nd ed.). Sage.

Helmefalk, M., & Hultén, B. (2017). Multi-sensory congruent cues in designing retail store atmosphere: Effects on shoppers' emotions and purchase behavior. *Journal of Retailing and Consumer Services, 38,* 1–11. https://doi.org/10.1016/j.jretconser.2017.04.007

Herships, S. (2016, Aug. 29). There are more adult diapers sold in Japan than baby diapers. Marketplace. https://www.marketplace.org/2016/08/09/world/japans-changing-culture

Hill, C. (2004). The psychology of rhetorical images. In C. Hill & M. Helmers (Eds.), *Defining visual rhetorics* (pp. 25–40). Lawrence Erlbaum.

Hofstede, G. (2001). *Culture's consequences.* Sage.

Holpuch, A. (2020, Sept. 18). "A lifesaver": US seniors turn to Zoom to connect with friends and family. *The Guardian.* https://www.theguardian.com/us-news/2020/sep/18/us-seniors-video-calls-zoom-coronavirus

Horan, S. (2021). Where retirees are moving—2021 edition. Smartasset. https://smartasset.com/financial-advisor/where-retirees-are-moving-2021

Horovitz, B. (2019, June 11). How baby boomers are redefining what "old age looks like." ABC News. https://abcnews.go.com/Health/baby-boomers-redefining-age/story?id=63630369

Hovland, C., & Weiss, W. (1951). The influence of source credibility on communication effectiveness. *Public Opinion Quarterly, 15*(4), 633–650.

Hu, Y., Wang, J., Nicholas, S., & Maitland, E. (2021). The sharing economy in China's aging industry: Applications, challenges, and recommendations. *Journal of Medical Internet Research, 23*(7), e27758–e27758. https://doi.org/10.2196/27758

Hubbell, P. (2014). *The Old Rush: Marketing for gold in the age of aging.* LID Publishing.

Hughes, K. (2020, March 17). Coronavirus has Boomers asking: Who are you calling elderly? *The Wall Street Journal.* https://www.wsj.com/articles/coronavirus-has-boomers-asking-who-are-you-calling-elderly-11584457650

Ilomäki, L. Paavola, S., Lakkala, M., & Kantosalo, A. (2014). Digital competence—an emergent boundary concept for policy and educational research. *Education and Information Technologies, 21*(3), 655–679. https://doi.org/10.1007/s10639-014-9346-4

Im, K. (2021, July 9). I struck gold on TikTok, and in life, with my Korean grandma. *The Seattle Times.* https://www.seattletimes.com/opinion/i-struck-gold-on-tiktok-and-in-life-with-my-korean-grandma/

Infoplease. (n.d.). Life expectancy by age, 1850–2011. Retrieved December 19, 2022, from https://www.infoplease.com/us/health-statistics/life-expectancy-age-1850-2011

Irvine, J. (2006). Selling Viagra. *Contexts, 5*(2), 39–44. https://journals.sagepub.com/doi/pdf/10.1525/ctx.2006.5.2.39

Jaffe, I. (2020, May 12). Coronavirus pandemic exposes cracks in nursing home system. NPR. https://www.npr.org/2020/05/12/854363905/coronavirus-pandemic-exposes-cracks-in-the-nursing-home-system

Jenkins, J. (2022, Jan./Feb.). Searching the world for better ways to age. *AARP Bulletin*, 38.

Ji, H., & Cooper, A. (2017). "Aging . . . the great challenge of this century": A content analysis of retirement communities' websites. Paper presented to the Association for Education in Journalism and Mass Communication annual conference, Chicago.

Ji, H., & Cooper, A. (2022). "Distorted mirror"? 20 years of elders' images in *Time* magazine advertising. *Atlantic Journal of Communication* (published online). https://doi.org/10.1080/15456870.2022.2117814

Ji, H., Cooper, A., Kanayama, T., & Gilliford, E. (2021). Sakazuki, Kodokushi: Website depictions of Japanese seniors in the world's grayest society. *Keio Communication Review, 43*, 23–42.

Johnson, C., Richmond, L., & Kivel, B. (2008). "What a man ought to be, his is far from": Collective meanings of masculinity and race in media. *Leasure/Loisir, 32*(2), 303–330.

Johnson, S. (2021a, May 2). Between 1920 and 2020, the average human life span doubled. How did we do it? Science mattered—but so did activism. *The New York Times Magazine*, 12–21, 54–61.

Johnson, S. (2021b, Oct. 8). How humanity doubled life expectancy in a century. TED talk. https://www.ted.com/talks/steven_johnson_how_humanity_doubled_life_expectancy_in_a_century?language=en

Johnston, E. (2016, Feb. 15). Kanazawa retirement community a relocation-from-Tokyo success story. *Japan Times*. https://www.japantimes.co.jp/news/2016/02/15/national/kanazawa-retirement-community-relocation-tokyo-success-story

KAF. (2020, March 23). 8 historical facts about *Time* magazine. https://www.kickass-facts.com/8-historical-facts-about-time-magazine

Kakulla, B. (2021). Personal tech and the pandemic: Older adults are upgrading for a better online experience. AARP Research. https://www.aarp.org/research/topics/technology/info-2021/2021-technology-trends-older-americans.html

Kantchev, G. (2021, Dec. 22). Aging Germany is running out of workers, putting Europe's largest economy at risk. *The Wall Street Journal*. https://www.wsj.com/articles/aging-germany-is-running-out-of-workers-putting-europes-largest-economy-at-risk-11640180607

Kendal. (n.d.). Kendal values. Retrieved January 3, 2023, from https://www.kendal.org/about-kendal/kendal-values

Kenigsberg, B. (2021, Jan. 14). *Some Kind of Heaven* review: Hardly an idle retirement. *The New York Times*. https://www.nytimes.com/2021/01/14/movies/some-kind-of-heaven-review.html

Khan, H. (2020, May 12). What is strategic communication? https://www.simpplr.com/blog/2020/what-is-strategic-communication

Kinsley, P. (1943). *The Chicago Tribune: Its first hundred years, volume 1, 1847–1865.* Knopf.

Kis, E. (2021, Dec. 5). Infographic: It's time to rethink Baby Boomers. *Ad Week*. https://www.adweek.com/brand-marketing/infographic-its-time-to-rethink-baby-boomers

Kolman, W. K., & Bartkowski, F. (2010). *Feminist theory: A reader* (3rd ed.). McGraw-Hill.

Kostev, K. (2020). Sex differences in people aging with HIV in Germany. *Journal of Acquired Immune Deficiency Syndromes* (1999), *84*(3), e11–e11. https://doi.org/10.1097/QAI.0000000000002349

Kotler, W. K., & Armstrong, G. (2014). *Principles of marketing* (15th ed.). Pearson.

Kramer, J., & Schreyogg, J. (2019). Demand-side determinants of rising hospital admissions in Germany: The role of ageing. *The European Journal of Health Economics*, *20*(5), 715–728. https://doi.org/10.1007/s10198-019-01033-6

Krekula, C. (2007). The intersection of age and gender: Reworking gender theory and social gerontology. *Current Sociology, 55*(2), 155–171.

Krout, J. A., Moen, P., Jolmens, H. H., Oggins, J., & Bowen, N. (2002). Reasons for relocation to a continuing care retirement community. *The Journal of Applied Gerontology, 21*(2), 236–256.

Kubota, M., & Babazono, A. (1997). Utilizing CCRC concept for long-term care policy of Japan. *Journal of Health Science, 19*, 31–40.

Lafayette, J. (2019). Top planners find audience buying an appealing approach. *Broadcasting & Cable, 149*(8), 14–23.

Law Insider. (n.d.). Nursing homes definition. https://www.lawinsider.com/dictionary/nursing-homes

LeadingAge. (n.d.). Our story. https://leadingage.org/our-story

Lei, L., Cooper-Chen, A., & Cheng, H. (2007). Advertising portrayals of the elderly in Chinese and U.S. elder-audience magazines. Paper presented at the Ohio Communication Association annual meeting, Boardman, OH.

Lemire, C. (2021, Feb. 19). I care a lot. Roger Ebert. https://www.rogerebert.com/reviews/i-care-a-lot-movie-review-2021

Liberty Lutheran. (2021). https://www.libertylutheran.org/social-services-philadelphia

Lim, Y. J. (2020). *Public relations: A guide to strategic communication*. Cognella.

Ling, Y., Song, Z., Yu, Y., & Jiang, T. (2021). Dealing with an aging China: Delaying retirement or the second-child policy? *PloS One, 16*(1), e0242252–e0242252. https://doi.org/10.1371/journal.pone.0242252

Lissitsa, E., & Kagan, M. (2022, March). The Silent Generation vs Baby Boomers: Sociodemographic and psychological predictors of the "gray" digital inequalities. *Computers in Human Behavior, 128*, 107098. https://doi.org/10.1016/j.chb.2021.107098

Llana, S. (2017, Jan. 2 and 9). Where seniors count. *The Christian Science Monitor Weekly*, 26–32.

Locke, C. (2022, May 25). "Grandfluencers" are sharing a new vision of old age. *The New York Times*. https://www.nytimes.com/2022/05/25/style/tiktok-old-gays-retirement.html

Luttner, K. (2017, Jan. 27). Coen Brothers direct a love letter to "*Easy Rider*" for Mercedes-Benz Super Bowl spot. Campaign Us. https://www.campaignlive.com/article/coen-brothers-direct-love-letter-easy-rider-mercedes-benz-super-bowl-spot/1422327

Macdonald, B. (1983). Look me in the eye. In B. Macdonald & C. Rich, *Look me in the eye, old woman* (pp. 25–41). Spinsters, Ink.

Manfred, E. (2021, Aug. 26). Too old for TikTok? Nope! SeniorPlanet. https://seniorplanet.org/seniors-tiktok

Mannheim, K. (1949). *Ideology and utopia: An introduction to the sociology of knowledge.* Harcourt, Brace.

Marcellus, J. (2008). Nervous women and noble savages: The romanticized "other" in 19th century U.S. patent medicine advertising. *Journal of Popular Culture, 41*(5), 784–808.

Martin, A. (2019, Nov. 16). The gray wave: Japan attempts to deal with its increasingly elderly population. *Japan Times.* https://www.japantimes.co.jp/news/2019/11/16/national/social-issues/gray-wave-japan-attempts-deal-increasingly-elderly-population/#.Xo08Z8hKjIU

Marx, K, A. , Burke, K. L, , Gaines, J. M., Resnick, B., & Parrish, J. M. (2011). Satisfaction with your new home: Advantages and disadvantages to living in a CCRC. *Seniors Housing & Care Journal, 19*(1), 83–96.

Maslow, A. H. (1954). *Motivation and Personality.* Harper & Row.

McAllister, B. (1998, Nov. 18). AARP alters name to reflect reality. *The Washington Post.* https://www.washingtonpost.com/archive/politics/1998/11/18/aarp-alters-name-to-reflect-reality/4340b2cb-b170-4cc7-9806-23dfebe3da8a

McCann Worldgroup. (2017). Truth about age. https://mccann1886.co.za/assets/files/documents/Truth-About-Age1.pdf

McConatha, J., Schell, F., & McKenna, A. (1999). Description of older adults as depicted in magazine advertisements. *Psychological Reports, 85*(3), 1051–1056.

McFall, L. (2015). *History of advertising.* Wiley.

McGuire, W. J. (1989). Theoretical foundations of campaigns. In R. E. Rice & C. K. Atkin (Eds.), *Public communication campaigns* (2nd ed., pp. 43–65). Sage.

McNamara, J., Lewin, M., Adi, A., & Zerfass, A. (2016). "PESO" media strategy shifts to "SOEP": Opportunities and ethical dilemmas. *Public Relations Review, 42,* 377–385. https://doi.org/10.1016/j.pubrev.2016.03.001

McWilliams, A. (2020, April 30). Getting back to normal: Lessons from a global crisis. *Psychology Today.* https://www.psychologytoday.com/us/blog/your-awesome-career/202004/getting-back-normal

Medicaid Interactive. (n.d.) Medicaid eligibility for Medicare beneficiaries who need long-term care in a nursing home. https://www.medicareinteractive.org/get-answers/cost-saving-programs-for-people-with-medicare/medicare-and-medicaid/medicaid-eligibility-for-medicare-beneficiaries-who-need-long-term-care-in-a-nursing-home

Meiners, N., & Seeberger, B. (2010). Marketing to senior citizens: Challenges and opportunities. *The Journal of Social, Political, and Economic Studies, 35*(3), 293–328.

Melo, M., Faria, V., & Lopes, A. (2019) Building professional identity: A study with female managers who are baby boomers, generation Xers, and millennials. *Aquatic Mammals, 45*(6), 832–843.

Metcalf, A. (2016). *From skedaddle to selfie: Words of the generations.* Oxford University Press.

Michas, F. (2022, March 3). Distribution of hospice patients in the U.S. by age, 2019. https://www.statista.com/statistics/339880/age-distribution-of-hospice-patients

Moore, P. (1986). *Disguised: A true story.* Word, Inc.

Morin, C. (2011). Neuromarketing: The new science of consumer behavior. *Society, 48*(2), 131–135. https://doi.org/10.1007/s12115-010-9408-1

Morrissey, J. (2017, Oct. 15). Baby Boomers to advertisers: Don't forget about us. *The New York Times.* https://www.nytimes.com/2017/10/15/business/media/baby-boomers-marketing.html

Moschis, G. P. (1992). *Marketing to older consumers: A handbook of information for strategy development.* Quorum Books.

Mule, D. (2015, March 2). 5 senior market segments and how to sell to them. Think Advisor. https://www.thinkadvisor.com/2015/03/02/5-senior-market-segments-and-how-to-sell-to-them/

Naoi, M. (1996). *Koreshi to kazoku* [The elderly and the family]. Saiensusha.

Navarro-Prados, Serrate-Gonzalez, S., Muñoz-Rodríguez, J.-M., & Díaz-Orueta, U. (2018). Relationship between personality traits, generativity, and life satisfaction in individuals attending university programs for seniors. *International Journal of Aging & Human Development, 87*(2), 184–200. https://doi.org/10.1177/0091415017740678

Nelson, M. (2018, May 24). Only 22% of CCRCs in the U.S. are for-profit. *Senior Housing News.* https://seniorhousingnews.com/2018/05/24/only-22-of-ccrcs-in-the-u-s-are-for-profit/

Nelson, R. A. (2015). Marketing: Communication tools. In W. Donsbach (Ed.), *The concise encyclopedia of communication* (pp. 336–337). Wiley.

New York Times. (1987, Aug. 12). Obituary: Clara Peller, the actress in "Where's the Beef?" TV ad. Section D, 22.

Nielsen. (2019). Introducing Boomers. https://www.nielsen.com/wp-content/uploads/sites/3/2019/04/nielsen-boomers-report-082912.pdf

Nonprofit Explorer. (n.d.). AARP. https://projects.propublica.org/nonprofits/organizations/951985500

Nyren, C. (2005). *Advertising to Baby Boomers.* Paramount Market Publishing.

Nyren, C. (2021, Sept. 12). Where's the beef? Advertising to Baby Boomers. http://www.advertisingtobabyboomers.com/2021/09/wheres-beef.html

O'Driscoll, A. (2021). Documenting the changing cultural values in TV advertising in Ireland from 1960s to 1980s. *Creative Industries Journal.* https://doi.org/10.1080/17510694.2021.1878668

Office of the United Nations High Commissioner for Refugees (UNHCR). (n.d.). Older persons. https://emergency.unhcr.org/entry/43935/older-persons#:~:text=An%20older%20person%20is%20defined,or%20age%2Drelated%20health%20conditions

O'Keefe, R. J. (2015). *Persuasion theory and research* (3rd ed.). Sage.

O'Meara, S. (2020). How health research will support China's ageing population. *Nature* (London), *578*(7793), S1–S3. https://doi.org/10.1038/d41586-020-00279-y

Otoo, F., Kim, S., Agrusa, J., & Lema, J. (2021). Classification of senior tourists according to personality traits. *Asia Pacific Journal of Tourism Research, 26*(5), 539–556. https://doi.org/10.1080/10941665.2021.1876118

Owler. (n.d.) AARP services. https://www.owler.com/company/aarp

Paek, H. J., & Shah, H. (2003). Racial ideology, model minorities, and the "not-so-silent partner": Stereotyping of Asian Americans in U.S. magazine advertising. *Howard Journal of Communication, 14,* 225–243.

Page, S. (2022). Marketing to seniors in 2022 (29 proven tips). Giant Partners. https://giantpartners.com/marketing-to-seniors

Paivio, K., & Csapo, A. (1973). Picture superiority in free recall: Imagery or dual coding? *Cognitive Psychology, 5,* 176–206.

Panko, B. (2017, Feb. 8). Where did the FDA come from, and what does it do? *Smithsonian.* https://www.smithsonianmag.com/science-nature/origins-FDA-what-does-it-do-180962054

Pasadeos, Y., & Renfro, R. B. (1992). A citation study of public relations research, 1975–86, *Public Relations Review, 15,* 48–50.

Paszak, P. (2020, Nov. 26). China is aging at a rapid pace. Warsaw Institute. https://warsawinstitute.org/china-aging-rapid-pace

PBS NewsHour Weekend. (2021, Oct. 10). YouTube. https://www.youtube.com/watch?v=Sgk4wt5aVfo

Pearce, B.W. (2007). *Senior living communities* (2nd ed.). Johns Hopkins University Press.

Petty, R. (2019). Pain-killer: A 19th century global patent medicine and the beginnings of modern brand marketing. *Journal of Macromarketing, 39*(3), 287–303.

Pew Research Center. (2015, Sept. 3). The whys and hows of generations research. https://www.pewresearch.org/politics/2015/09/03/the-whys-and-hows-of-generations-research

Pew Research Center. (2017, May 17). Technology use among seniors. https://www.pewresearch.org/internet/2017/05/17/technology-use-among-seniors

Pieczka, M. (2019). Looking back and going forward: The concept of the public in public relations theory. *Public Relations Inquiry, 8*(3), 225–244. https://doi.org/10.1177/2046147X19870269

Pinsker, J. (2020, Jan. 27). When does someone become 'old'? *The Atlantic.* https://www.theatlantic.com/family/archive/2020/01/old-people-older-elderly-middle-age/605590

Pollay, R. (1986, April). The distorted mirror: Reflections on the unintended consequences of advertising. *Journal of Marketing, 50,* 18–36.

Pollay, R., & Gallagher, K. (1990). Advertising and cultural values: Reflections in the distorted mirror. *International Journal of Advertising, 9*(4), 359–372.

Poon, L., & Holder, S. (2020, May 6). The "new normal" for many older adults is on the Internet. *Bloomberg News.* https://www.bloomberg.com/news/features/2020-05-06/in-lockdown-seniors-are-becoming-more-tech-savvy

Population Reference Bureau. (2021). Countries with the oldest populations in the world. https://www.prb.org/resources/countries-with-the-oldest-populations-in-the-world

Pornpitakpan, C. (2004). The persuasiveness of source credibility: A critical review of five decades' evidence. *Journal of Applied Social Psychology, 34*(2), 243–281.

Porter, R. (2003). *Blood and guts: A short history of medicine.* W.W. Norton.

Prieler, M., & Kohlbacker, F. (2016). *Advertising in the aging society: Understanding representations, practitioners and consumers in Japan.* Palgrave Macmillan.

Public Relations Society of America (PRSA). (n.d.). About Public Relations. https://www.prsa.org/about/all-about-pr

Purtill, C. (2021, Dec. 8). The key to marketing to older people? Don't say "old." *The New York Times.* https://www.nytimes.com/2021/12/08/business/dealbook/marketing-older-people.html

Quantum Wellness Botanical Institute. (2020, June 1). https://www.ftc.gov/legal-library/browse/cases-proceedings/172-3131-quantum-wellness-botanical-institute-llc

Raman, P., Harwood, J., Weis, D., Anderson, J., & Miller, G. (2008). Portrayals of older adults in U.S. and Indian magazine advertisements: A cross-cultural comparison. *The Howard Journal of Communications, 19,* 221–240. Doi: 10.1080/10646170802218214

Regan, T. (2019, March 29). Brightview CEO: We must avoid "big company mentality" while gaining scale. *Senior Housing News.* https://seniorhousingnews.com/2019/03/29/brightview-ceo-we-must-avoid-big-company-mentality-while-gaining-scale

Rich, M., & Inoue, M. (2021, Nov. 15). A new source of fuel in an aging Japan: Adult incontinence. *The New York Times.* https://www.nytimes.com/2021/11/15/world/asia/adult-diapers-japan.html

Ritchie, H. (2019, May 23). The world population is changing. Our World in Data. www.ourworldindata.org.

Robinson, H. (n.d.). Housing options for older adults: A guide for making housing decisions. The National Association of Area Agencies on Aging. https://www.n4a.org/files/HousingOptions.pdf

Robinson, R., Keyes, K. M., Martin, C. L., & Yang, Y. (2013). Birth cohort effects on abdominal obesity in the United States: The Silent Generation, Baby Boomers and Generation X. *International Journal of Obesity, 37*(8), 1129–1134. https://doi.org/10.1038/ijo.2012.198

Roy, A., & Harwood, J. (1997). Underrepresented, positively portrayed: Older adults in television commercials. *Journal of Applied Communication Research, 25,* 39–56.

Runciman, D. (2018, Aug. 20). Democracy's aging problem. *Time,* 221–222.

Sanger, D. (2021, March 11). The lessons of one of the worst years in American life. *The New York Times.* https://www.nytimes.com/2021/03/11/us/politics/biden-coronavirus-trump.html

Scharlach, A., Graham, G., & Lehning, A. (2011). The "Village" Model: A consumer-driven approach for aging in place. *The Gerontologist, 52*(3), 418–427. doi: 10.1093/geront/gnr083

Schlomann, A., Bünning, M., Hipp, L., & Wahl, H.-W. (2021). Aging during COVID-19 in Germany: A longitudinal analysis of psychosocial adaptation. *European Journal of Ageing,* 1–10. https://doi.org/10.1007/s10433-021-00655-1

Schon, M., & Stahler, N. (2020). When old meets young? Germany's population ageing and the current account. *Economic Modelling, 89,* 315–336. https://doi.org/10.1016/j.econmod.2019.10.034

Scott, D. (2016, March 21). The FDA wants to know how well older people understand TV drug ads. https://www.statnews.com/2016/03/21/fda-drug-ads-tv-older-populations

Scott, E. (2022, April 13). Two Florida men at The Villages admit to voter fraud in 2020 election. *Washington Post.* https://www.washingtonpost.com/politics/2022/04/13/florida-voter-fraud-2020

Sellnow, T. L., & Seeger, M. W. (2021). *Theorizing crisis communication* (2nd ed.). John Wiley.

Shalal, A. (July 12, 2021). Aging population to hit U.S. economy like a "ton of bricks"—U.S. commerce secretary. Reuters. https://www.reuters.com/world/us/aging-population-hit-us-economy-like-ton-bricks-us-commerce-secretary-2021-07-12

Shavitt, S., Lowrey, P., & Haefner, J. (1998). Public attitudes toward advertising: More favorable than you might think. *Journal of Advertising Research, 38*(4), 7–22.

Sherman, S. (1997). Images of middle-aged and older women: Historical, cultural and personal. In J. M. Coyle (Ed.), *Handbook on women and aging* (pp. 14–28). Greenwood.

Shmerling, R. (2021, March 22). FDA curbs unfounded memory supplement claims. *Harvard Health Blog.* https://www.health.harvard.edu/blog/fda-curbs-unfounded-memory-supplement-claims-2019053116772

Shoemaker, P., & Reese, S. (1996). *Mediating the message* (2nd ed.). Longman.

Simpson, M., & Cheney, G. (2007). Marketization, participation, and communication within New Zealand retirement villages. *Discourse & Communication, 1*(2), 119–222.

Slusher, M., Mayer, C., & Dunkle, R. (1996). Gays and lesbians older and wiser (GLOW): A support group for older gay people. *Gerontologist, 36*(1), 118–123.

Smith, L. (2022, Jan. 10). 12 digital marketing trends that will define 2022 (according to the experts). Local iQ. https://localiq.com/blog/2022-digital-marketing-trends

Smith, S., Choueiti, M., & Pieper, K. (2017). *Over sixty, underestimated: A look at aging on the "silver" screen in best picture nominated films.* Media, Diversity & Social Change Initiative at USC's Annenberg School.

Solomon, M. (2020, Jan. 10). What Millennial and Gen Z customers can teach you about everyone else. Chief Executive. https://chiefexecutive.net/what-millennial-and-gen-z-customers-can-teach-you-about-all-your-customers

Sommer, M. (2020, Jan. 4). Breaking through the barrier of digital complexity. *Elm Magazine.* https://elmmagazine.eu/adult-education-and-mature-learners/breaking-through-the-barrier-of-digital-complexity

Sompocare. (2019). About. https://recruit.sompocare.com/about/company

Southeast Discovery. (n.d.). 78 million baby boomers—what are they thinking? http://www.southeastdiscovery.com/78-million-baby-boomers.php

Stallings, S. (1992). From printing press to pharmaceutical representative: A social history of drug advertising and promotion. *Journal of Drug Issues, 22*(2), 205–219.

Statista. (2021). Share of old age population (65 years and older) in the total U.S. population from 1950 to 2050. https://www.statista.com/statistics/457822/share-of-old-age-population-in-the-total-us-population

Statista. (2022). Median household income by race or ethnic group 2020. https://www.statista.com/statistics/1086359/median-household-income-race-us

Stobbe, M. (2021, May 5). US birth rate falls to lowest point in more than a century. Associated Press. https://apnews.com/article/birth-rates-science-coronavirus-pandemic-health-d51571bda4aa02eafdd42265912f1202

Stock, K. (2022, March 19). Robot truckers could replace 500K U.S. jobs. *Bloomberg Business News Daily.* https://www.bnnbloomberg.ca/robot-truckers-could-replace-500k-u-s-jobs-1.1739921

Studdon, J. (2017, March 4). Elasticity of belief. *Psychology Today.* https://www.psychologytoday.com/us/blog/adaptive-behavior/201703/elasticity-belief

Sudo, C. (2021, Oct. 8). New projects, data show how Covid is reshaping senior living adaptive reuse market. *Senior Housing News.* https://seniorhousingnews.com/2021/10/08/new-projects-data-show-how-covid-is-reshaping-senior-living-adaptive-reuse-market

Sukkwai, Kijroongrojana, K., Chonpracha, P., Pujols, K. D., Alonso-Marenco, J. R., Ardoin, R., & Prinyawiwatkul, W. (2018). Effects of colorant concentration and "natural colour" or "sodium content" claim on saltiness perception, consumer liking and emotion, and purchase intent of dipping sauces. *International Journal of Food Science & Technology, 53*(5), 1246–1254. https://doi.org/10.1111/ijfs.13704

Tahmincioglu, E. (2021, May 3). Boomers buying food for parents, cars for kids. *Today.* https://www.today.com/money/boomers-buying-food-parents-cars-kids-750946

Taylor, E. (2012, Dec. 4). An aging "Quartet," still polishing their legends. NPR https://www.npr.org/2012/12/04/166447254/an-aging-quartet-still-polishing-their-legends

Thabit, M. (2015, June 8). How PESO makes sense. *PR Week.* https://www.prweek.com/article/1350303/peso-makes-sense-influencer-marketing

Tretheway, A. (2001). Reproducing and resisting the master narrative of decline: Midlife women's experiences of aging. *Management Communication Quarterly, 15*(2), 183–226.

Tully, T. (2021, Feb. 23). This 105-year-old beat COVID. *The New York Times.* https://www.nytimes.com/2021/02/23/nyregion/new-jersey-lucia-declerck-covid.html

Tumin, R., & Bogert, J. (2021, March 14). One year in a pandemic: Your weekend briefing. *The New York Times.* https://www.nytimes.com/2021/03/14/briefing/one-year-in-a-pandemic.html

United Health Foundation. (2021). America's health rankings senior report. https://www.americashealthrankings.org/learn/reports/2021-senior-report/introduction

United Nations. (2019). World population ageing 2019. Department of Economic and Social Affairs. https://www.un.org/en/development/desa/population/publications/pdf/ageing/WorldPopulationAgeing2019-Highlights.pdf

U.S. Census Bureau. (May 2014). The Baby Boom cohort in the United States: 2012 to 2060. https://www.census.gov/prod/2014pubs/p25-1141.pdf

U.S. Census Bureau. (2020). Current Population Survey, Annual Social and Economic Supplement, 2019. https://www2.census.gov/programs-surveys/cps/techdocs/cpsmar19.pdf

U.S. News & World Report. (2015). Boomers are valuable consumers who make informed life decisions to carry them into their next phase of life. https://www.usnews.com/pubfiles/USNews_Market_Insights_Boomers2015.pdf

Vernimmen, T. (2021, May 11). Why do older individuals have greater control of their feelings? *Smithsonian Magazine*. https://www.smithsonianmag.com/science-nature/why-do-older-individuals-have-greater-control-their-feelings-180977693

Vespa, J. (2019). The U.S. joins other countries with large aging populations. U.S. Census Bureau. https://www.census.gov/library/stories/2018/03/graying-america.html

The Village at Penn State. (n.d.). Who is Liberty Lutheran? https://www.retireatpenn state.org/liberty-lutheran-retirement-pa

WARC. (2020, Oct. 14). How Viagra's repositioning brought unexpected benefits. https://www.warc.com/newsandopinion/news/how-viagras-repositioning-brought -unexpected-benefits/en-gb/44221

Wee, S., & Myers, S. (2020, Jan. 16). China's birth rate hits historic low, in looming crisis for Beijing. *The New York Times*. https://www.nytimes.com/2020/01/16/busi ness/china-birth-rate-2019.html

Werner, J., & Mower, J. (1986). Source credibility: On the independent effects of trust and expertise. In R. Lutz. (Ed.), *Advances in Consumer Research, Volume 13* (pp. 306–310). Association for Consumer Research.

Wilson, S., & Modi, P. (2015). Personality and older consumers' green behaviour in the UK. *Futures, 71,* 1–10.

Witte, K., & Allen, M. (2000). A meta-analysis of fear appeals: Implications for effective public health campaigns. *Health Education & Behavior, 27*(5), 591–615.

Wolf, K., & Archer, C. (2018). Public relations at the crossroads: The need to reclaim core public relations competencies in digital communication. *Journal of Communication Management, 22*(4), 494–509. https://doi.org/10.1108/JCOM-08-2018-0080

World Bank. (n.d.a). Population ages 65 and above, total. https://data.worldbank.org/indicator/SP.POP.65UP.TO?most_recent_value_desc=true

World Bank. (n.d.b). Population total. https://data.worldbank.org/indicator/SP.POP. TOTL

Xie, Q., Neill, M. S., & Schauster, E. (2018). Paid, earned, shared and owned media from the perspective of advertising and public relations agencies: Comparing China and the United States. *International Journal of Strategic Communication, 12*(2), 160–179. https://doi.org/10.1080/1553118X.2018.1426002

Xue, F., & Ellzey, M. (2009). What do couples do? A content analysis of couple images in consumer magazine advertising. *Journal of Magazine and New Media Research, 10*(2), 1–17.

Yanni, D. (1990). The social construction of women as mediated by advertising. *Journal of Communication Inquiry, 14*(1), 71–81. Doi: 10.1177/019685999001400107

Ylanne, V., Williams, A., & Wadleigh, P. M. (2009). Ageing well? Older people's health and well-being as portrayed in UK magazine advertisements. *International Journal of Ageing and Later Life, 4*(2), 33–62.

Yoon, C., Cole, C., & Lee, M. P. (2009). Consumer decision making and aging: Current knowledge and future directions. *Journal of Consumer Psychology, 19*(1), 2–16. doi: 10.1016/j.jcps.2008.12.00

Young, J. H. (1961). *The toadstool millionaires: A social history of patent medicines in America before federal regulation.* Princeton University Press.

Index

Page references for figures are italicized.

AARP, 28–29, 31, 51–52, 121
AARP The Magazine, 27, 28, 31, 79, 97
Adams, John, 65
Adams, Michael, 119
advertising: ethics of, 67, 68; gender portrayals in, 111–14; medical, 63–79; minority portrayals in, 112–14; seniors' portrayals in, 51–62
Affleck, Ben, 29
African American elders. *See* Black elders
ageism, xi, 8, 110
agencies (advertising), 51, 53
aging: attitudes about, 126; social implications of, 1. *See also* economic impact of seniors
Aibo, 11
ailments, 65, 73, 123
Akins, Tom, 24
Alabama, 26
Alzheimer's Association, x, 4, *57*
appeals used in advertising, 52, 65, 72, 77, 87
Arizona, 24, 95, 116
Asian elders, 111–15
assisted living, 19–22

Baby Boomers, 4, 5, 6, 8, 83; economic power of, 7, 114; in Florida, 96, 97; in Germany, 129; social media use by, 86, 89. *See also* Facebook; technology
behavioral change, 45
Benioff, Marc, 55
Biden, Joe, 4
birth rates, 128–30
Bishop, Bojinka, 33
Black elders, 111–15
bloodletting, 56
Boomers. *See* Baby Boomers
Boudreau, Martha, 29
Bradley, Michelle, 19
branding, 25, 68, 76, 84
Buffett, Jimmy, 95
businesses, age-related, 2–3. *See also* assisted living; Continuing Care Retirement Communities; nursing homes

California, 37, 70, 76, 77, 116, 138
careers, ix, 17–32
CARF. *See* Commission on Accreditation of Rehabilitation Facilities
CCRCs. *See* Continuing Care Retirement Communities
China, 10, 68, 128
cholera, 77
cinema. *See* films
Colorado, 38, 39, 43, 47, 118, 138

comedies, 135
Commission on Accreditation of
    Rehabilitation Facilities (CARF),
    99–100
communication, 69. *See also* media
    relations; public relations
community relations, 32
Conley, Chip, 51
Connecticut, 96, 116
consumerism in seniors, 7, 125
contingency theory, 37–38, 44
Continuing Care Retirement
    Communities (CCRCs), 22–25,
    98–99; and COVID, 33–47; website
    marketing by, 99–106
COVID, 9, 26, 33–47, 89, 114–15
crises, 26, 37–38, 46

Dailey, Deborah, 26
dating, 126, 131
Dau, Jim, 28
Davis, Lisa, 28
death. *See* mortality
DeClerck, Lucia, 33
demographics, 87, 95, 110, 127
DeSantis, Ron, 26
digital competence, 130. *See also*
    technology
disease. *See* ailments
distorted mirror (advertising theory),
    53–55
Dole, Bob, 88
Donley, Susan, 26
drugs, advertisements for, 66–79
Ducker, Marilyn, 19
Dychtwald, Ken, 51

economic impact of seniors, 6, 8, 24,
    114, 121, 124
effects, societal, 121
Egypt, 68
Eisenhower, Dwight, 4
Elderhostel. *See* Road Scholar
elderist theory, 109, 114

elderly, 8. *See also* aging; Baby Boomers;
    gerontology
external communication, 44, 46–47

Facebook, 9, 84, 132
FDA. *See* Food and Drug Administration
fear appeals. *See* appeals used in
    advertising
Federal Trade Commission (FTC),
    64–65, 78
feminism, 110–11
Fengler, Wolfgang, 123
films, 135–36
Finland, 127
Florida, 24, 26, 27, 32, 37, 53, 95, 96,
    97
Fonda, Henry, 91
Fonda, Jane, 92, 109
Fonda, Peter, 87
Food and Drug Administration (FDA),
    63–64, 78, 79
Franklin, Ben, 65
FTC. *See* Federal Trade Commission
futures, study of, 122–23

Garland, Judy, 91
gay elders. *See* LGBTQ elders
gender portrayals, 111–15
generational cohorts, 4, 132
Gen. X, 6, 132
Gen. Z, 6, 132
Georgia, 76
Germany, 128–30
gerontology, ix, 121
Glenn, John, 4
global aging, 127–30
Glover, Madison, 23
The Golden Girls, 92
golfing, 95
Google, 89
Grace and Frankie, 91–92, 109, 119
graphics, 75, 76
Greece, 127
Green, Sheila, 109

Hadden, Briton, 54
hair restorative, ads for, 72–75
Hawaii, 116
Hepburn, Katherine, 91
hierarchy of needs (Maslow), 100, 103, 105
Hispanic elders, 111–15
Hong Kong, 130
hospice, 30–31
housing, 12, 97, 114–15. *See also* assisted living; Continuing Care Retirement Communities
Hubbell, Peter, 52

Illinois, 37, 70, 76
image restoration theory, 37
immigrants, 10
India, 127
industries, age-related, ix. *See also* businesses
internal communication, 46–47
internet, 13, 25. *See also* technology
invisibility of older women, 109, 111. *See also* marginalization of older women
Irving, Paul, 1
Italy, 13, 127

James, Emily, 28
Japan, 10–13, 68, 127
Jefferson, Thomas, 65
Johnson, Steven, 1, 65
Jones-Alexander, Staci, 121
Journal of the Economics of Ageing, 95

Kansas, 24, 38, 39, 91, 118
Keaton, Diane, 91
Kimura, Jiroemon, 10
King, Matthew, 17

LeadingAge, 25–27, 35
legislation, 24, 27, 28
LGBTQ elders, 118–19
Likins, Gretchen, 29, 84, 116, 118
Locke, John, 72

longevity, 10, 65
long-term care. *See* nursing homes
Louisiana, 53
Luce, Henry, 54

Maine, 138
Mannheim, Karl, 5
marginalization of older women, 109–10
market segmentation, 85, 123–26
marketing, 6–8; deceptive, 78; definition of, xi; localized, 20; to retirees, 97–106; role of emotions in, 85–86; shift in, 87
Maryland, 19, 21
Masiello, Julie, 21
Massachusetts, 116, 137
Maurer, Heather, 30
McKnight's Long-Term Care News, ix
media relations, 25, 26, 27, 44
Medicaid, 18, 28
Medicare, 18, 28
Medill, Joseph, 72
messages, definition of, xi; effective, 86; for senior marketing, 83–91, 97
Mexico, 10
Michigan, 96
millennials, 6, 7, 132
minority elders, 112. *See also* Asian elders; Black elders; Hispanic elders
Mississippi, 116
Missouri, 76
Moore, Pat, 109
Morrow, Linda, 23
mortality, 29–30, 65
Musk, Elon, 87
Musk, Maye, 87
Mussotto-Conyers, Cheri, 43, 46

naturally occurring retirement communities (NORCs), 98
Netflix, 96, *See also Grace and Frankie*
neuromarketing, 85–86
newspapers, 65, 69–77; criticism of, 67; *Press and Tribune* (Chicago), *71*

Nicholson, Jack, 91
NORCs. *See* naturally occurring
   retirement communities
Nottingham, Diedra, 119
Nevada, 8, 53, 116
New Hampshire, 84
New Jersey, 33, 138
New Mexico, 138
New York, 69, 76, 99, 118, 119, 138
North Carolina, 24, 25, 31, 38, 39, 43,
   45, 95, 118
North Dakota, 2
nursing homes, 17–19
Nyren, Chuck, 51

Ohio, 17, 18, 30, 31, 32, 37, 38, 39, 40,
   43, 47, 118
old age, stereotypes of, 7
Oregon, 38, 39, 40, 42, 43,46, 115, 118

Page, Steve, 87
pandemic. *See* COVID
Parsons, Alanna, 23, 43, 45
Peller, Clara, 51
Pennsylvania, 23, 24, 37, 38, 39, 41, 118
Perri, Kelsey, 83
persuasion: advertisers' use of, 67–68;
   marketers' use of, 84
PESO model, 90
Poehler, Amy, 29
politicians, older-aged, 4
Pollay, Richard, 53
Portugal, 127
press release, COVID-related, 133–34
Prevagen, 63–64
products, senior-oriented, 10–11, 121.
   See also businesses
public relations, definition of, xi
Public Relations Society of America, 35
publications, 27, 35
publics, 31
puffery, 78

racial portrayals, 112–17
Reagan, Ronald, 1

Redford, Robert, 87
regulations, 68. *See also* legislation
retirement communities, 95–106. *See
   also* Continuing Care Retirement
   Communities
Revere, Paul, 66
Road Scholar, 3, 83–84
robots, 10, *11*

sales, xi, 31
Sanders, Lisa, 18, 26, 35
Sanger, David, 47
segmentation of markets. *See* market
   segmentation
services for seniors, 122
Shaw, Donald, 66, 70
Sheen, Martin, 92, 119
Shmerling, Robert, 63
Silent Generation, 5, 6
silver (metal), 1
Singapore, 127
situational crisis communication, 37
Social Security, 4
Soltis, Julie, 43, 45, 47
source credibility, 32, 97, 105
South Carolina, 97
Stark, Maggie, 39, 43, 46
stereotypes, senior-related, 7, 8, 9
strategic communication, 124–27;
   definition of, xi. *See also* advertising;
   marketing; public relations
Studdon, John, 45
super-aged societies, 127–30

Tanaka, Kane, 10, 13
technology, 9, 121, 130–32. *See also*
   robots
Tennessee, 76
terminology, 8, 83–84
Texas, 53, 70, 76
Tik Tok, 90, 132
time, seniors' perspectives on, 124–25
Time magazine, 54–61, 95; minorities
   portrayed in, 112–14; gender
   portrayals, 112–14

Tomlin, Lily, 92, 109
Traditionalists. *See* Silent Generation
Trump, Donald, 1
tsunami, 1
Tuma, Nadia, 126
Turkey, 68
Tyler, Anne, 3

United Kingdom, 127
United Nations, 4
United States, 1, 13, 127

Van Der Linden, Nick, 26
Via, Angie, 21, 32
Viagra, advertising campaigns for, 87–89
Virginia, 18, 19, 28, 31, 32, 70, 72, 77, 115, 116

Washington, DC, 25, 28, 29, 111, 116
Washington, George, 66
Waterston, Sam, 92, 119
wealth of seniors, 123, 124, 132
websites, 24, 44, 89, 99–106, 114–18
West Virginia, 18
widowhood, 116
Wiley, Harvey, 65
Wyoming, 37
Wythe, George, 66

young people, 10

Zoom, 45, 131

About the Authors

Anne Cooper worked for 10 years full time as a journalist, magazine editor and public relations practitioner before beginning a 26-year teaching career at Ohio University. During that career, she was the graduate director at the E.W. Scrips School of Journalism. A Fulbright Senior Research Scholar in Japan and a DAAD scholar in Germany, she has written/coauthored/edited five previous books and numerous journal articles. Her work has been featured in the Sunday *New York Times,* on ABC-TV, the BBC and other media outlets.

Young-Joon Lim is associate professor in the Department of Communication at the University of Texas, Rio Grande Valley, where he teaches courses in mass media campaigns, theories of communication, research in communication, and public relations theory and practice. Lim has experience in insurance sales, news reporting and public relations for the defense industry. He is author of *Public Relations: A Guide to Strategic Communications* (2nd ed., 2021).